Beautiful and Terrible Things

Beautiful and Terrible Things

A Christian Struggle
with Suffering, Grief, and Hope

CHRISTIAN M. M. BRADY

WESTMINSTER
JOHN KNOX PRESS
LOUISVILLE · KENTUCKY

© 2020 Christian M. M. Brady

First edition
Published by Westminster John Knox Press
Louisville, Kentucky

20 21 22 23 24 25 26 27 28 29—10 9 8 7 6 5 4 3 2 1

Unless otherwise indicated, Scripture quotations are from the New Revised Standard Version of the Bible, copyright © 1989 by the Division of Christian Education of the National Council of the Churches of Christ in the U.S.A., and are used by permission.

Book design by Drew Stevens
Cover design by Nita Ybarra

Library of Congress Cataloging-in-Publication Data

Names: Brady, Christian M. M., author.
Title: Beautiful and terrible things : a Christian struggle with suffering, grief, and hope / Christian M.M. Brady.
Description: First edition. | Louisville, Kentucky : Westminster John Knox Press, 2020. | Summary: "When his eight-year-old son died suddenly from a fast-moving blood infection, Brady heard the typical platitudes about accepting God's will and knew that quiet acceptance was not the only godly way to grieve. With deep faith, knowledge of Scripture, and the wisdom that comes only from experience, Brady guides readers grieving losses and setbacks of all kinds in voicing their lament to God, reflecting on the nature of human existence, and persevering in hope"-- Provided by publisher.
Identifiers: LCCN 2020022299 (print) | LCCN 2020022300 (ebook) | ISBN 9780664266127 (paperback) | ISBN 9781611649987 (ebook)
Subjects: LCSH: Suffering--Religious aspects--Christianity. | Grief--Religious aspects--Christianity. | Hope--Religious aspects--Christianity.
Classification: LCC BV4909 .B729 2020 (print) | LCC BV4909 (ebook) | DDC 248.8/66--dc23
LC record available at https://lccn.loc.gov/2020022299
LC ebook record available at https://lccn.loc.gov/2020022300

Dedicated to
John William McKenzie "Mack" Brady
16 January 2004 ✠ 31 December 2012

Rest eternal grant to him, O Lord,
and let light perpetual shine upon him.
May his soul, and the souls of all the departed,
through the mercy of God, rest in peace. Amen.

CONTENTS

INTRODUCTION

MY GOD

I had forgotten that it was New Year's Eve. I called the president of our university, the man who had hired me and become my mentor, to tell him that our son Mack was being taken by helicopter to Hershey Medical Center. I asked if I could have the number of the dean of the School of Medicine to ask him for any assistance. When the dean answered the phone, I could hear the party in the background.

Elizabeth and I drove the two and half hours south from State College to Hershey, not knowing that Mack had already died on the helicopter, almost before we had left town. We found out the next morning that it was sepsis, a fast-moving blood infection that has a 50 percent mortality rate if properly diagnosed within an hour or two of onset, over 90 percent if not caught immediately. It presents itself like the flu—in Mack's case, the same flulike symptoms that his buddy had two days before. Within thirty-six hours of waking up with a fever, our little boy, my buddy, was gone.

When we arrived at the hospital, we were escorted to the ironically named "quiet room" and told the chaplain

1

would be with us soon. I knew what that meant, and I told my wife. I won't pretend to remember the details and order of events; it remains an emotional, swirling vortex of trauma in my mind and body even seven years later. Self-consciously, I admit that when we heard that Mack had died, the very first thing that came to my mind was to scream out,

My God, my God, why have you forsaken me?
   Why are you so far from helping me, from the words
   of my groaning?

I swallowed the words. I kept them inside me because it seemed melodramatic, too sanctimonious, to utter them aloud. But they came unbidden—and can you really be "melodramatic" standing by the body of your child? Silently, in my mind, the words continued to run again and again through my head as we stood next to his lifeless form.

How could God turn his back to us? How could it be that Mack was gone, our prayers ignored? We had prayed with Mack as they put him on the gurney to take him on his first and last ride in a helicopter. As it took off, we looked up from the parking lot, and I wept as I prayed, "Lord! Protect my child!" In that room, I wanted to wail, and I wept. At times I continue to wail, and I suppose these words are an extension or a continuation of that wailing. Even now, years later, every day we cry some, and some days we cry a lot.

O my God, I cry by day, but you do not answer;
   and by night, but find no rest.

These opening verses of Psalm 22 are a lament of one surrounded, literally or metaphorically, by enemies, but the emotion they contain, the despair, is felt by any who grieve. Yet every time I find myself invoking this psalm, part of my mind immediately chastises me, saying, "Who are you to invoke the words of Christ?" I am a person in pain, grieving, that is who. These were Jesus' words, but first they were the words of the psalmist. Jesus appropriated them, and so can we.

A few years after his son Eric died, Christian philosopher Nicholas Wolterstorff published a collection of essays and reflections called *Lament for a Son*.[1] I have often noted the lack of an article. He does not offer "a lament" or "the lament" for a son. He implores us to "lament for a son"—his son. This is *my* lament for *my* son.

Lament is, at its heart, personal. Even when we lament as a community, we each bring our own voice to the chorus. This work is also then, out of necessity, a reflection on my own life. I grew up in the church being taught from the earliest age the Scriptures that would eventually form the foundation of my faith as well as the basis of my academic discipline. And in that horrible moment when we stood over Mack's beautiful, lifeless body, it was Scripture that came to mind: "My God, my God, why have you forsaken me?"

CHAPTER 1

LETTING IT OUT

In the hospital, in the hours after our son had died, I restrained myself and refrained from crying out. Yet in my head the noise was deafening. "How! How could you let this happen? How could he be gone? Gone. Here but not. Present but forever absent. Gone." But we held each other, my wife and I, and we cried over Mack's little body. We remained quiet, in shock, stoic.

Everyone reacts to death differently and grieves differently. I learned that when I was barely a teenager. When my grandfather died it was noted by the family that, even though we were all very close, I did not cry. His daughters and wife each responded in various ways. None better or worse than the other except in the eyes of those who felt hurt that the other was not showing enough respect, or love, or decorum. This added hurt to grief that continues to this day, over thirty years later. In grief, some will cry, some will wail, some will sit still silently. An important truth to establish at the outset of this book is that we need to leave ourselves and others room to grieve, to grieve without judgment of ourselves or others.

Yet oddly enough, many Christians are told that they should *not* grieve. Sadness is selfish, some say, since your child/wife/friend is whole and safe with God. Let your mourning turn into dancing! To grieve is to lack faith in the resurrection! Do you really believe? Then you will be happy for those who "sleep in the Lord"!

Less than two weeks after Mack died, I posted a brief essay on my blog about whether Mack's death was God's will, a topic I will turn to shortly. One commenter on my blog challenged me. "You should ask yourself: where is your child better off? In heaven now or alive and suffering the many situations that bring pain and suffering to him? If you say the latter then I would say you are being self-ish in your thinking."[1] Many readers came to my defense, but I was not surprised or hurt by this person's comment. I understood that it came from a well-intended (if curt) effort to encourage me to focus on the promise of the resur-rection that we have in Jesus. I was equipped to respond to such comments, since it was a subject I had already thought long and hard about, yet I have since spoken to many grieving parents who have received the same mes-sage from their church communities. This sort of misplaced "faith" devastated them, precisely when they most needed spiritual support.

As is so often the case, such well-meaning but mis-guided sentiments come from a misreading of Scripture, in this case 1 Thessalonians 4:13. Paul is encouraging the believers at Thessalonica and helping them to place their grief in the context of their new faith: "But we do not want you to be uninformed, brothers and sisters, about those who have died, so that you may not grieve as others do who have no hope."

Paul is not telling them that they should *not* grieve; rather, he is encouraging all those who believe in Christ that their grief not need be as those "who have no hope."[2] We *will* grieve; that is a given and should not be rushed past or diminished. Our knowledge of the resurrection, our faith that the kingdom of God will be established and that we will be reunited with God and our loved ones, does not remove our feelings of loss and sorrow *now*. Those who try to rush past this time of lamentation are robbing themselves and others of the necessary expression of grief. Furthermore, we are encouraged by the Word of God, both Scripture and the Word made flesh, to lament, to cry out, and even to express our anger.

Grief, it must be noted, does not only come with the death of a loved one; we grieve all sorts of things in our life. Often, however, we do not realize or acknowledge that our response to the loss of these things, such as the breakdown of a marriage or a change in career, is actually grief. Under my photo in my high school yearbook is the statement "MD or bust!" When I entered high school I was determined to become a research physician. When I introduced myself to others during freshman orientation at college, I would offer the usual orientation greeting: hometown, major, and extracurricular: "I am from DC; I am a chemistry major, pre-med; and I am on the swim team." It was my identity, expressed in strong "I am" statements. I "was" those things. By the time Thanksgiving break arrived, however, I had quit the swim team and was no longer a chemistry major; visions of medical school and the white lab coat had evaporated. What followed were several years of depression and confusion as I stumbled along, trying to figure out who I was going to be and what I was going to do. I know now that I was grieving, grieving the loss of my identity as a swimmer and budding physician. There is much that could be said about not placing one's identity and self-worth in such external things as a career and activities, but for this discussion it is important to note that my grief was real, and it needed to be treated as such. That possible future I had envisioned was gone, and I needed the time and space to reflect and acknowledge the new life that lay before me.

There is a wonderful little volume called *Good Grief* by Granger Westberg. Originally a chapter within a larger work reflecting on Westberg's time in ministry as a Lutheran pastor on the faculty of the University of Illinois Medical School, *Good Grief* is now past its fiftieth year and remains a thoughtful and empowering guide to grieving and caring for those who grieve. I was given this book by a friend, my spiritual director and former pastor, when Mack died. It was there that I first came across the observation that in 1 Thessalonians Paul is not telling us that we should not grieve, but rather that we should grieve in a way different from those who do not know the hope of the resurrection.

It was also in that little book that I realized how many different things we grieve. "A list of losses would be inexhaustible," says Westberg. "We can lose our health, our eyesight, our hearing. . . . In some families grief comes with the loss of a pet which has been a part of everything that has gone on in that household for ten years or more. . . . To say a person is deeply religious and therefore does not have to face grief situations is ridiculous. Not only is it unrealistic, but it is also incompatible with the whole Christian message."[3] There are so many things in life that we will grieve, that we ought to grieve, not least the very nature of our world, as we shall see in the next chapter. The message of Scripture is that God is redeeming us *and* the world. It is an ongoing process and requires our full participation with God, experiencing the sorrows and suffering of this world as well as the joy, love, and comfort found in the grace of God.

Honest to God

Not long ago, a friend wrote to let me know that he and his wife were filing for divorce. They are kind and loving parents and had been very thoughtful and careful about making their decision. He concluded by writing, "I feel it would be an appropriate time to reread Job, but I don't want to wallow, only to grieve and rebuild my own self step-by-step." My friend understands that he has embarked on a long process, a grieving process, and that the book of Job is a good place to begin reflection.

Job is often the first biblical book people turn to when they experience some loss or catastrophe in their lives. It is understandable, as it opens with Job losing just about everything in his life in a short span of time. His children and their families are killed, his massive flocks and herds are killed or stolen, and his body is overcome by painful and debilitating sores. Famously, Job's friends come to offer him comfort and support by challenging him repeatedly to simply admit his guilt, for he must have sinned in *some* way (and it could not be in any small way either, given the results), and accept God's punishment. Job, however, knows that he has done nothing to deserve this treatment and remains firm in his statement of innocence and demand for God to speak to him, to explain his suffering. He stands for all of us who have felt the world collapse on us for no discernible reason.

The audience knows the explanation for his suffering because we have the preface (Job 1:6–12) in which God and "the Adversary," *haśatan*, place a bet on whether or not Job will remain faithful to God in the face of such incredible hardship.[4] Scholars debate the dating and structure endlessly, but it is perhaps best to understand the work as an effort to think through the problem of suffering and our usual responses to it.[5] For this "thought experiment" to work, the audience needs to know that Job is in no way deserving of his fate, and the preface provides that certainty to us, a certainty that Job possessed but his friends knew nothing about. Job is also presented as a kind of "everyman." He is not an Israelite or member of any other tribe that we know of, he is not a patriarch or hero of the Israelite tradition, and he is from the "land of Uz," which cannot be located with any certainty. Job is someone who can represent any one of us in any place or time, experiencing the vicissitudes of life.

As the book of Job cycles through the friends' exhortations, Job himself remains resolute; he is innocent. Yet he is not silent: "Therefore I will not restrain my mouth; I will speak in the anguish of my spirit; I will complain in the bitterness of my soul" (Job 7:11). His friends would have him confess and repent, but Job insists on being honest with God. We will return to these disputes later; it is the honesty and integrity of Job that is important to note here. Confronted with crippling loss and illness, Job will not keep quiet; he speaks and insists that God take note of his plight, to see his situation and deliver him. This is not the action of an arrogant or prideful man but of a faithful person. It is a holy and healthy part of grief (that we seem to have forgotten) to express to God our sadness, our anger, and our bitterness. When we are in the midst of our anguish, there is no greater statement of faith than to express that despair honestly: "My God, why have you forsaken me?"

Yet far too often we are told that it is never right to be angry at God.[6] We are told we must have "an attitude of gratitude" and praise God for all that we have, even the hardship, because "suffering produces endurance." Frequently devotional books and sermons are like Job's friends, adjuring us to consider the weight of our sins and the justice of God's punishment without taking into account the suffering that is not punishment, the anguish that comes from unjust hardship. Job addresses that anguish, provides us with an example to follow, and gives us the permission to say to God, "Do not condemn me! Let me know why you contend against me" (Job 10:2).

It is not that Job's friends, or the sermons and devotional books of today, are not in some way right. In fact, that is the very point of the poetic dialogues in the book of Job: they represent the usual biblical response to suffering, primarily that suffering is often the consequence of sin or God's loving reproof. Our lived experience, however, testifies that often we experience loss and tragedy for which we bear no responsibility. Mack's death was not deserved in any way. Neither he nor we, his parents, sinned such that death would be the appropriate penalty, not in God's law or in our limited human justice. So Job is an exemplar for us. He knows he is innocent; we know he is innocent; and sometimes *we know we are innocent*. In the face of this reality, the platitudes and calls to repentance ring hollow and, far from bringing comfort, only exacerbate the wounds. "Your maxims are proverbs of ashes," says Job (13:12). They provide no sustenance or nourishment, only bitterness.

It is vital that we are honest with God and ourselves, especially during times of great struggle and pain. That honesty requires us to bring all of our emotions to our divine relationship, letting it all out, our praise *and* our pain. This is why a majority of the psalms are psalms of lament. They are honest expressions of grief and models of prayer. It is not surprising that in his darkest and deepest moment Jesus invoked a psalm of lament to express his anguish, pain, and fear. We often are reminded that Jesus was "without sin" while forgetting that he was also human, like us, and "in every respect has been tested as we are" (Heb. 4:15). In his human experience Jesus wept. Jesus cried out to God. He grieved.

Jesus Wept—So Can We

Jesus grieved for his friend Lazarus, for the world, for himself. Even knowing the great value and gift of the sacrifice he was offering, even knowing that he would be raised from the dead just three days later, even knowing all this Jesus asked God, if possible, that he might be spared the suffering. Finally, in his last moments, he cried out in lament, "My God! My God! Why have you forsaken me?" If Jesus can challenge God, if Jesus can weep and grieve and ask God to spare him the pain and hardship, then so can we. So should we.

Jesus' cry, quoting the first words of Psalm 22, is perhaps one of the most challenging passages in the Bible (see Matt. 27 and Mark 15). Not only is the entire scene gut-wrenching—with Jesus beaten, stripped, and hanging from the cross while his mother and friends stand beneath him watching his anguish in anguish of their own—but this great cry of despair should penetrate our very souls. We see and cannot comprehend the physical suffering, and then we question even the theology of it. How is it that God could have forsaken himself? How could he forsake his Son?

The short answer is that God did not and would not. Just as we are human, Jesus was fully human and, in his humanity, experienced both the physical and spiritual horrors of this moment. Jerry Irish, reflecting on the death of his own young son and looking to the Gospels, finds Jesus just as frightened and appalled as we are by death. He grieves the death of others and even his own. Obedient though Jesus is, Irish writes, "the Gospel writers picture Jesus preparing for death as something dreadful. In Gethsemane, Jesus asks his closest disciples to be with him in his time of sorrow and trouble. 'Horror and dismay came over him.' Jesus said to his disciples, 'I am deeply grieved, even to death' (Mark 14:34)."[7] Even for the savior of the world, death is grievous, and Jesus expressed his full range of emotions toward God.

Jesus poured out his grief on the Mount of Olives shortly before he was betrayed:

> He came out and went, as was his custom, to the Mount of Olives; and the disciples followed him. When he reached the place, he said to them, "Pray that you may not come into the time of trial." Then he withdrew from them about a stone's throw, knelt down, and prayed, "Father, if you are willing, remove this cup from me; yet, not my will but yours be done." (Luke 22:39–42)

In his prayer Jesus gives us permission to ask God to spare us the difficult times. We are not called to be stoic soldiers, silently accepting whatever hardship comes upon us. We are allowed to ask for mercy, to be spared the suffering. Jesus utters this imperative to his disciples twice in this one passage, and it is, of course, the same prayer that we utter in the Lord's Prayer: "Save us from the time of trial, and deliver us from evil." So we too are allowed to ask God to spare us trials, tests, and difficult times, just as we are allowed to confront God with our grief and demand that he respond: "O my God, I cry by day, but you do not answer!"

If Jesus teaches us this, then I think it is safe to conclude that we are not being "spiritual wimps" when we pray for God's grace to ease our lives. A vital element of such prayer is our faith and willingness to accept such trials if God so desires, but we must be authentic with God even, and especially, in our darkest and deepest moments of fear and doubt.

Jesus' appeal to God on the cross is not, as it may seem, a cry of doubt or uncertainty, asking why God had abandoned him; rather, Jesus is invoking the entirety of the psalm, a psalm that is both a cry of lament *and* a confession of faith in God.[8] In Psalm 22, the psalmist calls out to God, demanding that God hear his cries of suffering and see the pain and hardship that he is enduring for the sake of his faithfulness, but it moves on in later verses to affirm the author's faith in God and confidence that God will save. Most of the psalms are just such laments, illustrating the importance of expressing our emotions fully and directly to God, not remaining in any one condition too long, but not holding back either.

Faith-Filled Lament

These psalms often begin with a "calling out" of God, a demand that God listen or a statement that God has rejected his people.

My God, my God, why have you forsaken me?
Why are you so far from helping me, from the words
of my groaning?
O my God, I cry by day, but you do not answer;
and by night, but find no rest.

—Ps. 22:1–2

Such language is jarring and often causes Christian read-ers to feel that the psalmist is impertinent if not heretical. Who are we to challenge God? And yet far from being blasphemous or a sign of faithlessness, it shows the depth of confidence that the psalmist has in God that the psalm-ist can call to the Lord and get a response. This is also the message of the book of Job. Job called on God and declared his innocence, and God responded. What the book of Job and the psalms of lament teach us, which we have often forgotten, is that we can and indeed must be sincere and honest with God. Our prayers should not be filled with platitudes and flowery language but should express our deepest needs and concerns, even our com-plaints against God. We are allowed to be angry with God, bitter and saddened by our life experience.[9] In so doing, we are giving our all to God, even our anger, disappoint-ment, and doubt.

When Jesus invokes this powerful psalm, he continues to show his faithfulness to God and his confidence in God's faithfulness to him. Within the heart of this psalm is an assertion:

Yet you are holy,
    enthroned on the praises of Israel.
In you our ancestors trusted;
    they trusted, and you delivered them.
To you they cried, and were saved;
    in you they trusted, and were not put to shame.

—Ps. 22:3–5

By invoking this psalm, Jesus declares that he knows it is God who will deliver him, the very God who has cared for him since birth and has guided his life. The psalm concludes with the confident assertion that God is ruler of all and will deliver the psalmist and his people:

All the ends of the earth shall remember
    and turn to the LORD;
and all the families of the nations
    shall worship before him.
For dominion belongs to the LORD,
    and he rules over the nations.

To him, indeed, shall all who sleep in the earth bow down;
    before him shall bow all who go down to the dust,
    and I shall live for him.
Posterity will serve him;
    future generations will be told about the Lord,
and proclaim his deliverance to a people yet unborn,
    saying that he has done it.

                      —Ps 22:27–31

This is the declaration of Jesus on the cross. It is not an expression of doubt as to whether God is still with him, but an acknowledgment that God is *always* present, even when it feels he is far from us and ignoring our pleas. It is an honest plea to God to see that Jesus is suffering and a confession that only God can save him. The same God who rescued Jesus' ancestors and has been his God since his mother bore him will deliver him and even all those who have gone down to the dust. It is a confession of faith in God even as it is an expression of grief.

    This is the example that Jesus provided in his last moments, in his darkest moments. So how do *we* lament? How can we be honest with ourselves and God while confessing our need for his saving grace? When we look at the psalms of complaint or lament, we find that they often have the same basic elements. Consider Psalm 13: There is an address or cry to God ("How long, O LORD? Will you forget me forever?" v. 1a) followed by a lament or complaint ("How long must I bear pain in my soul, and have sorrow in my heart all day long? How long shall my enemy be exalted over me?" v. 2). There follows a confession of trust ("But I trusted in your steadfast love; my heart shall rejoice in your salvation," v. 5) with an invocation calling God to action ("Consider and answer me, O LORD my God!" v. 3a). The psalm concludes with a vow to praise God ("I will sing to the LORD, because he has dealt bountifully with me," v. 6).

What we find is not just a literary device, but a healthy model for our own journey through grief: cry to God, lament, confess our faith, call God to action, and praise God. The psalms themselves show great variety in language and form, so we do not need to be bound to this structure, but the elements provide guidance and, for those who need it, permission to express our suffering and loss.

Our response to hardship and grief does not need to be pious silence; outrage and anger are acceptable! God is big enough and can handle our frustration and bitterness. Most importantly of all, God wants our honesty, so that we can be honest with ourselves. God wants us to share all of our selves, including our pain, and God wants to be present with us *in* our suffering, *through* our suffering.

Almighty God, whose most dear Son went not up to joy but first he suffered pain, and entered not into glory before he was crucified: Mercifully grant that we, walking in the way of the cross, may find it none other than the way of life and peace; through Jesus Christ our Lord. Amen.[10]

Reflection Questions

1. Read a few psalms of lament, such as Psalms 3, 13, 17, 57, and 86. Create your own lament, following the model: cry to God, lament, confess our faith, call God to action, and praise God.
2. How do you normally grieve and respond to death? How do you respond to death differently from people you know well?
3. What message do you think your faith community conveys to those who grieve? What do you think it means to grieve as those who have hope?
4. Think of a time when you grieved not because someone had died but because you had lost something, such as a job or dream or relationship. How is that grief similar to and different from grieving a death?
5. How do you feel when you consider that Jesus cried out to God or grieved the death of his friend Lazarus?

CHAPTER 2

HERE IS THE WORLD

*The grace of God means something like: "Here is your life.
You might never have been, but you are, because the party
wouldn't have been complete without you. Here is the world.
Beautiful and terrible things will happen. Don't be afraid.
I am with you. Nothing can ever separate us. It's for you
I created the universe. I love you."*
—Frederick Buechner, *Beyond Words*

This is Frederick Buechner's definition of "grace." I had
often heard, read, and even spoken those central words,
"Here is the world. Beautiful and terrible things will happen. Don't be afraid." It is a perfect quote for a graduation
ceremony, that time when we are sending young women
and men out into a world full of challenges and struggles.
We want to provide a warning along with encouragement:
"Life is hard and full of difficulties, but don't be afraid!
It is also a place of beauty and wonder and joy." This is
also where we must begin any study of the biblical understanding of suffering and grace, with the acknowledgment

that the world is both beautiful and terrible, glorious and dangerous.

After Mack died, I had more than a few days when my response to those gracious enough to ask how we were doing was simply, "It is what it is." This is such a trite phrase that we hear all the time. People utter it when they are enduring a hardship or, just as often, when there is a problem they would rather not deal with. It is what it is. Often devoid of any real meaning and all too often intended as a justification for inaction, the phrase is only slightly more articulate than the monosyllabic "Meh," accompanied by a shrug of the shoulders. "It is what it is. What can you do? It is what it is." It is the ultimate inarticulate dodge of responsibility.

Yet it is a phrase I now say with some regularity because of its deep, theological truth. Rather than an excuse not to think or act, "it is what it is" is an accurate expression of the condition of the world. As Buechner writes far more beautifully, "Here is the world. Beautiful and terrible things will happen." Accepting this reality of our broken world is the precondition to emotional and spiritual survival in this world.

This is not, of course, what the world was meant to be. When God created the world, he looked at all that he had made and saw that "it was very good." Chapters 1 and 2 of Genesis tell us that God created humanity to live in, protect, and enjoy this perfect world. Part of that perfection was allowing humanity the freedom to love and obey. With that came the possibility of disobedience as well. We all know the story, so I don't need to embellish it any further. We, humanity, succumbed to the desire to become wise, to be like God, knowing good and evil. Once the woman and the man, who was with her, took of that fruit, the world was forever changed. What was good and perfect is now broken, filled with pain, inequality, thorns and thistles, infections and cancer. This is the world that we live in — not the perfect garden, but a world of suffering, hardship, and injustice. It is the world that God created and that we transformed—a beautiful and terrible world.

"It" Happens

When Mack died, suddenly and without any warning, from the blood infection that went through him like a lightning strike in a tinder-dry forest, everyone sought to understand how it could happen—not just the medical reasons (there was no clear evidence of how he was infected, no cuts or scrapes), but the theological as well. How can God allow this to happen to an innocent child?

My upbringing and later extensive biblical and theological study had prepared me as well as anyone could be for the loss of a child—which is to say, not well enough. It is utterly devastating. Nothing can prepare you for the loss of your child. Yet because of all that study, I knew that we were not alone; I knew that such death was a part of this world. Throughout most of history and around the world, it was more common for children to die young than to achieve adulthood. A hundred years ago, over a third of all children did not even live beyond age five.[1] The Bible depicts the death of children (2 Kgs. 4:20) and of mothers in childbirth (Gen. 35:16–20) as the normal occurrence in life that it is. Our daughter's birth was very difficult and, had we not been in a developed country with modern medical facilities to allow a Cesarean section to be performed, it probably would have resulted in the death of both my wife and daughter. It is with good reason that the prophets and Paul refer to the chaotic and traumatic of this life, building toward the day of God's judgment, as "the whole creation . . . groaning in labor pains" (Rom. 8:22). Nor is it surprising that in the only two occasions when an actual woman is described in the Bible as crying out in labor, she dies in childbirth.[2] It is the nature of this world.

I learned all of this through the vicissitudes of life and more than a decade spent studying Lamentations. The five poems of this small biblical book graphically describe the impact of the Babylonian siege of Jerusalem. The poet cries out to God, "Look, O LORD, and consider! To whom have you done this? Should women eat their offspring, the children they have borne?" (Lam. 2:20). The poems are full of the horrors of warfare, starvation, greed, guilt, and regret. Just two weeks before Mack died of the infection, twenty children and six teachers and administrators were gunned down at Sandy Hook Elementary School—wanton destruction that neither those children nor their families deserved. These are the realities of this world, natural and sinful. The same man who said that we were selfish to want our son to still be here, in this world with us, rightly asked, "Why do parents think their child is immune to the rules that govern this life?" The truth is, I did not think that my children were immune, but that did little to assuage my grief.

All of this leads us to what theologians call *theodicy*, a branch of theology that questions the "justice of God" and defends the goodness of God in the face of evil—evil, like a child dying, or millions starving due to a drought or genocide, or the entire history of the world. How do we reconcile our belief in a good, just God with the injustice that is our reality?

When I was younger, my brain seemed to have little difficulty in maintaining two seemingly contradictory ideas. I believed what I had been told, that God had created the world and that human sin had allowed suffering and hardship to enter in. I believed also that God could and would answer our prayers and provide miraculous healing. As I grew older, experience taught me that prayer did not always yield the answers I so desperately wanted. I began to feel this inexorable drive to harmonize and systematize everything, not least of which were my beliefs.

This drive to systematize seems to be ubiquitous if not universal. I have observed that so much of Western Christianity, in particular the Reformation and its descendants, has been driven by a deep desire to bring all Scripture, belief, and teaching into one unified and consistent teaching. It does seem that our Orthodox brothers and sisters (of their various types) seem much more comfortable with ambiguity, in allowing the Trinity, for example, to be "true" without needing to explain the inner mechanics of the relationship between the Father, the Son, and the Holy Spirit. By contrast, the traditions within which I grew up and have since adopted are constantly trying to codify and organize Christianity, like Einstein seeking his unified theory of everything.

I have often quipped that I do not espouse or teach systematic theology because the Bible is not systematic. This is nowhere more true than in the case of suffering and grace. We are taught that God loves us and will answer our prayers by sending healing and deliverance from oppression, on the one hand. On the other, we are taught that the Bible clearly describes this very real world we live in, full of unjust and unmerited hardship, accusation, and death. The efforts to place all of this into a nice, tidy framework are never satisfying because they do not take into account the full testimony of the Bible or our lives.

The evidence of both views—God's loving, life-giving grace and the real suffering of this world—is not contradictory but real. The moment we place greater weight on one, we are diminishing the power, validity, and truth of the other. Today I am both profoundly happy and proud— of my wife, our daughter, and our son—but I am also deeply saddened; I feel the weight of the loss of Mack on my chest every minute of the day. What I feel in the depths of my being—the joy and the sorrow, the happiness and the grief—is the reality of this world. That is the truth, the tension of life. I experience the joy and revelry of seeing our daughter grow and flourish and also the deep, abiding sadness that our son grows no longer in this world. Both are true, both are reality, and both occur within this world that God created and that humanity transformed.

The Limits of Knowing

This is where I think we must begin and return, to stare firmly and fixedly at the true nature of this world and come to terms with the fact that it is what it is. If we are so fixed on the resurrection and the life of the World to Come, we can struggle to live in the world that is. The author of the book of Ecclesiastes took on that challenge and examined the life lived in this world. What he found, in the absence of God, was a world of hardship and routine where comfort and joy were fleeting and ephemeral, where all was like the merest breath.

Ecclesiastes, like Job, is a "thought experiment," in this case an examination of what our experience and perception of life might be if we omit the possibility of God. The Teacher, "Qohelet" in Hebrew, wrestles with the fundamental question of life: If things never change—the sun rises and the sun sets, people live and die, and everything is "vanity" or meaningless—then what is the purpose?

> Vanity of vanities, says the Teacher,
> vanity of vanities! All is vanity.
> What do people gain from all the toil
> at which they toil under the sun?
> —Eccl. 1:2–3

When we are in the midst of our own suffering and grief, when the sunrise follows sunset and we can't even remember the events of the evening before because we walk in sorrow, this refrain becomes our own.

Ecclesiastes is a compact book and can easily be read in less than an hour. In fact, you can read it on the short flight from Philadelphia to State College, Pennsylvania, as I did once while preparing to teach. If you are not a great flyer (I am always just that little bit anxious), then it may not be the most placid or calming of reads, but a little turbulence certainly focuses the mind on matters mortal.

Reading this book can be both a challenge and a comfort. It is comforting, to me at least, in that it offers an incredibly straightforward and unremittingly honest look at the world we live in. I have worked hard day after day, seen people hungry and dying, seen the wicked prosper and the righteous suffer, and the next day I get up to find that nothing has changed. I can relate more readily to Ecclesiastes than I can to Daniel in the lion's den. To read this in the Bible, our sacred Scripture, affirms my own life experience as legitimate and, well, normal. This is why, the Teacher tells us, he "applied [his] mind to seek and to search out by wisdom all that is done under heaven" (Eccl. 1:13). It is also a challenging work in that the answer, at first glance at least, seems to offer little comfort. But I shall return to that shortly.

Qohelet wants to apply human experience, knowledge, and wisdom to the question of purpose, to understand what is the meaning of life. (It would be millennia before Douglas Adams would suggest "42" as the answer to that particular question.) So he sets out to test life in all its experience, from frugality and excess, to the joy of food and folly, to the "delights of the flesh and many concubines." There are many twists and turns, reflections and complications in Qohelet's thoughts through the course of the work, but in the end he finds it was all fleeting and evanescent: "Vanity of vanities, says the Teacher; all is vanity" (Eccl. 12:8).

The Hebrew *hevel* is often translated as "vanity," as here in the New Revised Standard Version, yet it means something more like "vapor" or "breath." As Robert Alter points out, "The seventeenth-century translators obviously had the Latin version in mind, with 'vanity' suggesting a lack of value, not self-admiration."[3] The sense of Qohelet's statement is that everything is so fleeting, like the wisp of breath that can be seen on a cold morning—there for a moment, visible yet intangible, and then gone. That is life. That is the value of all our endeavors. The author returns time and again to this refrain, that after considering all of life's experiences, everything is "the merest breath."[4] Qohelet examines it all and finds that, whether it is the blessings of good health, food, and drink or the hardships of work and hunger, in the end all things pass away.

True, Ecclesiastes does not appear on the surface to be the most uplifting of books, and it is understandable that an agnostic like Bart Ehrman finds Qohelet to be "a biblical author I can relate to."[5] The power of the book is in the fact that the author is so unflinching in his gaze at life. The human experience is described well and succinctly: "Again, I saw all the oppressions that are practiced under the sun. Look, the tears of the oppressed—with no one to comfort them! On the side of their oppressors there was power—with no one to comfort them" (Eccl. 4:1). Human history is replete with such suffering; there is no need for me to recount it here; you can add your own experience to the litany, I am sure. And Qohelet articulates well the fate even of those blessed in this life. There are "those to whom God gives wealth, possessions, and honor, so that they lack nothing of all that they desire, yet God does not enable them to enjoy these things, but a stranger enjoys them. This is vanity; it is a grievous ill" (Eccl. 6:1–2).

Where is the comfort, then, in the book of Ecclesiastes for those who seek solace? Is it some sort of sick mistake to include it in the canon of the Bible? Is it really completely at odds with the rest of the so-called Wisdom literature of the Bible? No, it is not at odds; rather, it is sounding a harmonic note, adding to the overall song of Scripture. Like a psalm of lament, Ecclesiastes gives voice to our real, lived experience. If all we read in the Bible were stories of miraculous healing and deliverance and of suffering that was always and clearly only due to sin, then it would not accurately reflect this world we live in. Qohelet's description of life is our own, but it is partial.

The work is, as I suggested above, a kind of thought experiment. Not only is Qohelet seeking to understand the meaning of life, but to understand it *solely* from the human perspective. Without any additional revelation, the life we experience is just as Qohelet describes. It seems an endless cycle with no value other than enjoying what we have while we have it. Although it is anachronistic to describe it as such, Ecclesiastes is a kind of humanist treatise. Yet Qohelet is not an atheist or even an agnostic. He accepts that God exists but confesses to not knowing the mind of God: "Just as you do not know how the breath comes to the bones in the mother's womb, so you do not know the work of God, who makes everything" (Eccl. 11:5). Even as the wise and knowledgeable Qohelet tallies up all that he has observed, the futility and fleeting nature of it all, he acknowledges his own limitations of knowledge as well.

We feel the limits of our knowledge most keenly at death. From our perspective, Qohelet notes, "the fate of humans and the fate of animals is the same; as one dies, so dies the other. They all have the same breath, and humans have no advantage over the animals; for all is vanity. All go to one place; all are from the dust, and all turn to dust again. Who knows whether the human spirit goes upward and the spirit of animals goes downward to the earth?" (Eccl. 3:19–21). Who knows indeed! God knows, of course, and it is a part of Qohelet's experiment to limit the domain of inquiry to only that which his mind and wisdom might perceive of what "is done under heaven" (Eccl. 1:13). With that limitation in place, he reasonably concludes, as we all must under those constraints, that we cannot know what happens when we die.

Yet knowing that God does exist, Qohelet concludes that "God *will* judge the righteous and the wicked, for he has appointed a time for every matter, and for every work" and that "God is testing [humanity] to show that they are but animals" (Eccl. 3:17–18, emphasis mine). In due time, God will bring justice, but when is not for us to know. In the meantime, we are to remain humble even as we enjoy our work with which we have been tasked and the fruits of our labor (Eccl. 3:22). The importance of enjoying this life should not be passed over quickly. Qohelet exhorts us, "Go, eat your bread with enjoyment, and drink your wine with a merry heart; for God has long ago approved what you do" (Eccl. 9:7). It is perhaps something those of us from Protestant backgrounds have lost sight of: we are also called to worship God through enjoying the good fruits and pleasures that God created and placed in our lives for just that purpose, to make us happy.

We also have a promise that Qohelet did not possess, situated as we are on the other side of the cross and the empty tomb. We have received the revelation of God incarnate in Jesus and the testimony of the resurrection from the disciples. Yet our knowledge and experience remain incomplete as well. We confess our faith in the resurrection, but we continue to see injustice where there should be justice, to experience loss and hardship, and we don't know when Jesus will come again to bring justice and healing to the world.

This admitted limitation of human knowledge seems a cop-out to some, and I can understand why it may not feel terribly satisfying. Ehrman, in talking about the poetic portions of Job, which takes a similar position to Qohelet, expresses frustration with this admission of ignorance: "If we don't understand God by human standards (which [God] himself has given), how can we understand him at all, since we're human? Isn't this explanation of God's justice, at the end of the day, simply a cop-out, a refusal to think hard about the disasters and evils in the world as having any real meaning whatsoever?"[6] The short answer is no. No, it is not a cop-out, since neither Job nor Ecclesiastes has avoided thinking "hard" about the suffering and evil in the world. Rather both are willing to admit the limits of their knowledge, examining the world from the human perspective and admitting that there are "beautiful and terrible things," even as God's grace is present in our lives as well.

What Has God Promised?

We find this in the Old Testament narratives expressed in a different way. The main figures experience life much as we do, with normal day-to-day activities of baking, working, and caring for family punctuated by occasional crises and loss. It can often seem like these stories are distant from our own — Abraham and his clan were nomadic shepherds, whereas most of us are likely to work in a building of some sort, an office, a warehouse, a school — but work is work. Famine, violence, and war are sadly as familiar today as they were in the times of the Bible. In the United States, our "famine" may be in the form of joblessness or having to live on the cheapest, and therefore often the least healthy, food we can find. But violence and war, child death and family in-fighting all remain common life experiences.

The presence of God can also seem to set the biblical stories apart. It is easy to get the impression that God is always talking with Abraham and giving him clear directions on what to do next in his life. Yet when we read the Bible carefully, we find that God is generally neither hanging out in people's tents having tea nor orchestrating every single moment of people's lives. There are wide swathes of life when God does not intervene. Consider Abraham. God speaks and acts directly several times in Abraham's life, yet there are years, decades actually, that go by with apparently no additional divine involvement.

Or consider the story of Esther, which is famous for being the only book in the Bible in which God is not mentioned at all. There seem to be no miracles or interventions other than the faithfulness of Esther and Mordecai. The entire Jewish population of the empire is about to be destroyed by Haman, and rather than an army of angels appearing, Esther uses her position in the palace to persuade King Ahasuerus to halt the execution of the plot. The message of Esther is that terrible things happen in this world and that God often works through those who are willing to stand against evil. For many of us, it is perhaps the most relatable of any book in the Bible.

Elizabeth has often shared that when she would pray with Mack, she would tell him that she knew God had a purpose for him. How can that be reconciled with his death? Was that the purpose? No. Although his death has led to dramatic changes in all our lives, including comforting others who have lost children, it would be a cruel God indeed who would take a child so that we might develop empathy. As brief as it was, Mack's life had purpose and meaning; he lived fully and with great joy. But that did not stop tragedy from intervening.

The biblical world reflects this real world that we live in, where the promises of God are in tension with the adversity of daily life. In the biblical story of Rebekah, God tells her clearly the destiny of her children, yet that does not protect them from their own choices. What was an assurance to Rebekah in her pain became a source of conflict and strife that tore apart her family. When she was pregnant with the twins Esau and Jacob, Rebekah was in such anguish that she asked the Lord to take her life there and then (Gen. 25:22). She knew all too well that women often died in childbirth. Rather than go all the way to childbirth only to die, she cried out to God, "If it is to be this way, why do I live?" God heard her appeal, her lament, and reassured her. God told her that "two nations are in your womb, and two peoples born of you shall be divided; the one shall be stronger than the other, the elder shall serve the younger" (Gen. 25:23). Notice that he did not tell her that *she* would live through childbirth, though she did; instead he promised that her *children* would live and thrive, even in conflict. Rebekah clearly kept these words close to her heart, and Jacob, the younger of the two, became her preferred son even as Esau became Isaac's most favored heir.

What God did not tell Rebekah was *how* it would come about that the younger should rule over the elder. We know the story of how "Esau despised his birthright" and sold his inheritance for a bowl of lentil stew. Then, as their father Isaac was aged, blind, and nearing death, Rebekah helped Jacob to deceive Isaac and steal Esau's blessing, the holy and powerful last gift that Isaac wanted to bestow upon his firstborn son. In this way, Jacob became the ruler over his elder brother. God had promised Rebekah that this would be the case, but God did not ordain that it should occur through treachery and deceit.

How do we know that it was not as God intended? Because the means were wicked, and the results were evil. After she aided him in deception, Rebekah never saw her beloved Jacob again because he had to flee from his brother. Deep-seated conflict and resentment between his descendants resulted. Jacob's reputation as a trickster preceded him so that his uncle and future father-in-law trapped him into marrying the eldest daughter Leah before he could marry Rachel, saying, "This is not done in our country—giving the younger before the firstborn" (Gen. 29:26). Most damning of all is that Jacob's own sons would deceive him as he deceived his father. He tricked Isaac by slaughtering a goat and putting on his brother's clothes. His sons tricked him into believing that his beloved Joseph was dead by killing a goat and sprinkling its blood over their brother's infamous cloak (Gen. 37:31).

Did God's promise that "the elder shall serve the younger" necessitate all this sin and suffering? Is it not conceivable that the all-powerful God we affirm in the creeds could bring this to fruition without deception and harm? Of course. If we insist that God planned for his blessing to occur in *this* way, then we have to believe that God ordained Jacob to lie and cheat and cause all the suffering that followed. One could, of course, produce an intellectual justification for that in order to maintain a position that God ordains every single action undertaken in history, yet the biblical account is much simpler and more forthright. Rebekah and Jacob decided not to wait for God but took matters into their own hands and suffered the repercussions. God's promises continue, Jacob was blessed, and he and his descendants became Israel. Yet that was in spite of human efforts, not because of them.

God often works in this world in subtle ways, without exercising total control and while allowing for our own willfulness. The Bible does clearly testify that there are moments when God miraculously intervenes, but that is the exception, not the norm. Most of Abraham's life was spent dealing with the daily troubles of work and hardship; his faith and obedience did not remove the impact of famine on his life. As C. S. Lewis points out, "That God can and does, on occasions, modify the behavior of matter and produce what we call miracles, part of the Christian faith; but the very conception of a common, and therefore, stable, world, demands that these occasions should be extremely rare."[7] God does indeed have a plan for all of us, our ultimate destination being to reside in God's love in the new heaven and earth, but the details remain largely up to us. When we do find God intervening directly and miraculously in our lives, we should not dismiss it as a coincidence but offer thanksgiving and rejoice! Yet do not be discouraged when those moments seem few and far between; it is the nature of living in this world, and God remains present with us.

The sovereignty of God, God's rule "over all that is seen and unseen," as we say in the Nicene Creed, is not generally in debate. What exactly the term "sovereignty" means, however, is hotly contested. To be clear, to say that a king is sovereign over a people is *not* to say that he controls every aspect of a person's life, but that he has *authority* over their lives and the affairs of the nation. In a biblical context, such rulers did indeed have absolute authority. A king or his emissary could enter a home and take whatever they wanted, even the life of the family's firstborn son. But they did not dictate every last detail of a person's life.

It is natural that we find such biblical analogies with human kings who had absolute authority as a means of expressing God's sovereignty. Many Reformed theologians, however, have extended the definition to mean that God has absolute *control*. No doubt they have been led by the myriad of biblical verses that tell us of God's direction and guiding hand in our lives, but that evidence does not require the conclusion that God controls every single moment, decision, action, and choice. At issue, particularly with respect to the problem of suffering, is the *extent* of God's interaction and direction of our lives. If, as some assert, God's sovereignty means that he controls *everything* that happens in our lives, then God is directly responsible for all suffering and all evil.[8] Allowing an agent, such as Satan or cancer, to execute the action does not absolve God for the responsibility of it any more than it would in a human court.

The biblical testimony is much more complicated and even seemingly contradictory. D. A. Carson refers to this concept as "compatibilism." He defines it this way:

> The Bible as a whole, and sometimes in specific texts, presupposes or teaches that both of the following propositions are true: 1. God is absolutely sovereign, but his sovereignty never functions in such a way that human responsibility is curtailed, minimized, or mitigated. 2. Human beings are morally responsible creatures—they significantly choose, rebel, obey, believe, defy, make decisions, and so forth, and they are rightly held accountable for such actions; but this characteristic never functions so as to make God absolutely contingent.[9]

God is not bound by us or our actions and decisions. God remains "sovereign," having authority over all things and in Scripture providing us with direction on how we ought to live our lives, but God allows humanity to have autonomy, to have agency, and to make our own decisions and have responsibility for those choices. God does not direct and manage "the motion of every atom," yet graciously God *may* intervene. In Christ, God did intervene for all humanity and for all time.

We live in the promise that God will be present with us even as we, God's people, face hardship, injustice, and suffering. Sometimes that suffering is of our making, but frequently it is not. Faith is the strength to walk forward in those times between. God appeared to Abram and said, "Get up and go!" Abram did, and God appeared to him several more times, but there was a lot of living in between, thousands of miles walked from Ur to Canaan to Egypt and back again.

We each have moments of grace in our lives, times when God speaks to us through others, through circumstances, and through opportunities. Remembering those moments helps us to move through the hard miles of life. But those miles can be *so* hard. Don't beat yourself up for not being perfectly grateful at all times. Don't fall into the lie that you are not allowed to be angry at God or to express your frustration and disappointment. Open yourself up to *all* of life—the beautiful and the terrible things—share openly and honestly with God, and know that while there is hardship there is also blessing, that where there is suffering there is also grace.

Almighty God, you created this world as a holy and good place for us to be in communion with you. Yet we have become separated from you and one another, and it grieves us. We experience sickness, hunger, and violence, and we mourn. Yet through this creation you have also revealed to us your love and reconciled us to you and the whole world through your Son, our Savior, Jesus Christ. Revive and refresh us, and grant us your peace through the grace of our Lord Jesus Christ and the presence of the Holy Spirit. Amen.

Reflection Questions

1. How does the knowledge that countless people throughout the millennia have suffered similar losses and pain affect the way you think about your own suffering?
2. Do you struggle to reconcile the belief in God's goodness with the reality of suffering in the world? How well do you live with the tension and mystery of never really knowing "why"?
3. Read Ecclesiastes 4. What wisdom do you glean from Qohelet's observations?
4. How do you think of God's sovereignty? If God is sovereign yet allows us to make our own way, how does that affect our choices?
5. When have you experienced God's voice or presence in your life? When have you felt God's absence? What "moments of grace" have you experienced recently, even in the midst of suffering?

CHAPTER 3

THE WHY OF
SUFFERING

On a bright, spring Sunday morning, I walked up the wide steps of the Sixteenth Street Baptist Church in Birmingham, Alabama, for worship. I was in Birmingham with a group of students from our university's leadership academy; we were on a tour of key sites from the civil rights movement, but I was initially alone. I did not think it appropriate to "assign" students to attend a worship service. As I climbed the steps, I was greeted warmly by women in large hats and men in suits and ties, and I was welcomed into the sanctuary by helpful members of the congregation. I sat and prayed. Eventually some students from my group joined me in the pew.

There were other groups of students in the church (not all teachers shared my reluctance to assign a worship service), and the pastor welcomed us all. The congregation is used to groups joining them for worship because their church is a holy and sacred place. On September 15, 1963, white supremacists detonated a mass of dynamite under the steps of this African American church, injuring twenty-two people and killing four girls. Addie Mae Collins, Cynthia Wesley, and Carole Robertson were all fourteen years old, and Carol Denise McNair was only eleven. They were in the basement changing into choir robes in preparation for the service when the blast tore through the building. The sermon that was never preached was titled, "The Love That Forgives."[1]

Fifty-three years later the pastor was preaching on Jeremiah. I wish I could tell you what portion of the prophet he was preaching on, or really anything about the sermon, but my memories are of thinking about the hatred that led to the bombing, the tragedy inflicted on this community, and the amazingly gracious continued presence of this congregation. Here, in this place of worship and peace, violence ripped their world apart. How does anyone put the pieces back together again? How is any theology robust enough to withstand the blast?

These sorts of horrific and traumatic acts not only bring physical and emotional damage, but they often reveal just how fragile and simplistic our beliefs are as we begin to ask the most difficult questions. The theological questions come to mind as quickly as the political and sociological ones. As I sat in the Sixteenth Street Baptist Church, I could only imagine the questions asked by those impacted by the attack as anguish and fear poured into their lives. Here they were ready to worship and to preach forgiveness, yet violence forced its way into this time and place of serenity. I suspect they felt not only physical insecurity but spiritual insecurity as well. The church, a place of worship, is called a "sanctuary" precisely because it ought to be a place of safety and security. Yet there, in the midst of worship, violence found them and took the lives of their family and friends. How could God possibly allow such a violation?

Such an attack, vicious and intended to bring terror into a community, is not unlike the inward violence that anyone may feel when they have lost someone they love. Even if it is the death of a parent after a long, well-lived life from an illness with a progression the doctors predicted, when they depart from us, we are wounded. And all too often that leaving is not a gentle passing. At every death we ask why. We want to know how it is that the God who created this world could allow so much suffering, not just of those who are gone, but for those of us who remain.

How can a loving God allow children to be blown up in their house of worship? How can a child be born with a disease destined to take their life only a few short years later? Why should some suffer physical and emotional abuse only to die alone? When we look at all the suffering around us, the questions pile up like kindling that could burn the world to the ground. And yet often we are urged to simply "accept God's will." Yet this was *not* God's will for us. This is *not* the world that God intended for us to live in, and so we *must* ask the questions. In demanding answers from God, like Job, even if we do not receive clear answers, we will find God.

As we search for answers, we must be aware that it is an exercise fraught with difficulty. This is because often there is no purpose or meaning to be found in the *arrival* of suffering in our lives. We often only find it in the journey *from* that place of meeting. We will turn to that process of walking through suffering in chapters 6 and 7. Now, let us look at what the Bible says about the source of our suffering, why it is that in this world both beautiful *and* terrible things happen.

The "Whys" in Scripture

In our search for answers in Scripture, we must be careful that we do not rest our understanding too firmly on only a few verses, isolated from their context. If we do not consider the entire testimony of the Bible, we will likely come to erroneous conclusions that might harm ourselves and others. We also need to be cautious that we are not so self-centered that we run the risk of reducing all our suffering and hardship to our personal experiences without considering the structural and corporate sin that is part of the fabric of our society. On the other hand, if we view all our hardship and suffering as emanating from the actions of others, we ignore our own responsibility and culpability. Yet it is also important that we not take upon ourselves fabricated burden and guilt; that only compounds the suffering. The reality we live in is one where harm results from individual *and* corporate action; the sins of the individual often cascade down through generations or radiate out into entire communities. Other terrible things, like our son's infection, have no clear cause at all. This is why it is imperative that we take all of Scripture into account while also reflecting on the testimony of others.

As Christians, we turn to the Bible and often find what seem to be very clear explanations. In the book of Deuteronomy, Moses tells the Israelites that if they do not obey the Lord's commands, "all these curses shall come upon you and overtake you" (Deut. 28:15). To some it seems clear that if we are experiencing "disaster, panic, and frustration" (Deut. 28:20), then it must be because we have sinned against God and are being punished. Yet in the New Testament, we find a very different explanation for our suffering.

Jesus said often that those who followed him would be blessed but also would suffer greatly: "Blessed are the poor in spirit . . . those who mourn . . . those who are persecuted for righteousness' sake . . . Blessed are you when people revile you, and persecute you, and utter all kinds of evil against you falsely on my account" (Matt. 5:3, 4, 10, 11). Paul also describes the blessing of the hardship endured for the sake of following Jesus: "For [God] has graciously granted you the privilege not only of believing in Christ, but of suffering for him as well" (Phil. 1:29). Reading only the New Testament, we can understand why one author wrote that "suffering is God's plan for Christians."[2] Such passages from the New Testament, and there are many, seem to suggest that *all* suffering is a result of following Jesus and is sent by God. Many pastors teach just that. After all, Paul tells us that "suffering produces endurance, and endurance produces character, and character produces hope, and hope does not disappoint us, because God's love has been poured into our hearts through the Holy Spirit that has been given to us" (Rom. 5:3–5). Often we find (or are taught) that the biblical reasons for our suffering boil down to this paradoxical pair of explanations: it is because we sinned against God or because we were faithful to God. Either way, we suffer.

Yet if we take into account the entire witness of the Bible and the broad scope of human experience, we realize that it is not so simple to categorize suffering as a result of either sin or persecution for the faith. Nicholas Wolterstorff describes this painful ambiguity well:

> To the "why" of suffering we get no firm answer. Of course, some suffering is easily seen to be the result of our sin: war, assault, poverty amidst plenty, the hurtful word. And maybe some is chastisement. But not all. The meaning of the remainder is not told us. It eludes us. Our net of meaning is too small. There's more to our suffering than our guilt.[3]

The meaning, the explanation of *why* we suffer, may indeed elude us, but when we are considering a healthy spiritual response to loss, there is value in the contemplation. If the pain and hardship we are enduring is of our own making, if it is a result of our sin, then we should confess it and address it. If we are persecuted and bullied because we profess Christ as Lord, then we must seek courage and strength in the knowledge that we suffer as our Lord did and we suffer with our Lord. But when we experience loss, grief, illness, and hardship through no fault of our own, when we experience "the remainder," then we should acknowledge

God's grace and presence in our lives. So from a biblical perspective, where does suffering come from?

The Result of Sin

G. K. Chesterton, in commenting on H. G. Wells's proposals of a Utopia, observed that one of the fundamental difficulties with such a proposal is that humans will always prioritize their own needs over those of others: "A permanent possibility of selfishness arises from the mere fact of having a self."[4] This is also a central teaching of Genesis regarding human nature, regardless of how one regards the historicity of the book. So much of the suffering in the world comes from our selfishness. From the moment the man and the woman are expelled from the garden, the biblical narrative immediately moves on to describe the continued frailty and folly of human arrogance and avarice, underscoring the fact that this is the constant background noise of life.

Cain becomes angry that God will not accept his offering and allows his anger to consume him. In spite of God's warning that he must control his anger (Gen. 4:6–7), he gives himself over to that sin and takes the life of his brother, Abel. Cain is exiled, and the farmer who brought forth fruit from the land is now "a fugitive and a wanderer on the earth."[5] The opening chapters of Genesis describe how God left humanity to develop on their own, with the result that "every inclination of the thoughts of their hearts was only evil continually" (Gen. 6:5). The generation of Noah, Sarah's jealousy of Hagar, Isaac's preference for Esau, Jacob's tricking of his father Isaac, and Jacob's sons using the same methods to lie to Jacob and get rid of their annoying little brother Joseph—these and so many other scriptural stories exemplify behavior we experience in some way in our own lives. Every day we see the fruits of such selfishness, envy, and greed. These episodes also describe how such actions not just bring judgment upon the sinner but can, and very often do, devastate the lives of others. In such cases, the cause-and-effect relationship between our sin and suffering seems clear, following the pattern described by Deuteronomy.

After encouraging Israel and assuring them that if they did all that God had commanded them to do they would be blessed, God further warns that "if you will not obey the LORD your God by diligently observing all his commandments and decrees, which I am commanding you today, then all these curses shall come upon you and overtake you" (Deut. 28:15). A rather sizable list of curses follows, including the all-encompassing "disaster, panic, and frustration in everything you attempt to do" (v. 20). It seems rather straightforward, and the narrative passages and the law are united in saying that when we sin there are consequences in our lives. On a certain level this is not controversial. If I were to begin to abuse my body with drugs or alcohol the effects would be obvious, not just to my body but to my relationships and my career. That behavior would have dire consequences in my life, and it would be my fault, the result of my sinful behavior. Yet I would also bring about the suffering of others, from family members I hurt to strangers I endanger; their culpability would simply be their proximity to me.

As simplistic as it may seem on the surface, we cannot ignore this source of hardship and suffering in our lives. We must acknowledge that sin, disobeying God's direction for our lives individually and corporately, is real and affects our lives in significant ways. Often we are acting and responding to the sinful behavior of others that has impacted our lives. For example, it is a tragic truth that victims of child abuse often become abusers themselves. Today, many describe these effects in social, psychological, or biological terms, and we need to address them on that level as well, and we may need the help and guidance of professional counselors, therapists, and physicians in order to overcome the impact of our negative behavior or that of those around us.

When we find that our suffering and hardship come from our own behavior, then a crucial first step is to acknowledge our culpability. If, for example, I am angry and abusive to my coworkers and as a result of my actions am fired from my job, then it is imperative that I acknowledge my role in creating that situation and the consequences. My anxiety and grief over having lost my job is still real, but self-reflection and prayer are needed as a part of the grieving and healing process. This is nothing new; we find it time and again in everything from ancient stories to modern sitcoms and movies, yet it is surprising how often we seek to place the blame for our circumstances outside of ourselves. The challenge is to find the balance—to take responsibility for those things we have done while letting go and forgiving others for their role in our hardship.

The life of King David is full of such examples of sin, consequence, and repentance. There are details, however, that are often overlooked that bear directly on how we respond to guilt, grief, and suffering. The eleventh chapter of 2 Samuel opens as the kingdom is secure. David's army has gone out to battle, but David has selfishly decided to remain at home. All that follows results from David avoiding his responsibilities as king and being bored. While lounging on the roof of his palace, "[David] saw from the roof a woman bathing; the woman was very beautiful" (2 Sam. 11:2).

The story is fairly well known and yet often misremembered. The woman that David sees is, of course, Bathsheba; after he sends for her, "he lay with her." It is important to note that it is unlikely that Bathsheba went willingly. She was married to Uriah the Hittite, and while it may be that she did not fight against the king and his men, we cannot avoid the fact that this banal euphemism, "he lay with her," should be read as "David raped her." This is not just adultery; it is a fundamental violation. This is violent and carnal sin, as is the way in which David deals with Uriah by sending him to his death at the front of the assault on Rabbah. It is a further reminder that Bathsheba suffered greatly, through no fault of her own. David did not control his own emotions and took advantage of his position and power over Bathsheba and forced her into a life fraught with hardship, intrigue, and grief.

We continue to see such abuse of power all around us today. Humanity has not changed in that respect. Fortunately, things are beginning to change with respect to those who have been violated being able to speak out and push back against those who have used and abused them. As we have seen in the #MeToo movement, women who have suffered trauma at the hands of powerful men are calling those men to account. Sadly, the Christian community is all too often at the center of such violations, highlighted through the #ChurchToo extension of #MeToo. Leaders who have been entrusted with the spiritual and physical care of others, not to mention the basic Christian calling to love our neighbors as ourselves, have exploited their positions to satisfy their own desires. That such base behavior is part of human selfishness may explain its origins but does not justify or excuse it. Across all denominations and traditions, it is a terrible indictment, but it is also an opportunity for repentance and transformation if we are willing to confront and be confronted.

It is likely that no one within the court felt they could challenge David. But God sends the prophet Nathan to confront David with his sin. He does not do so directly but uses a parable. The prophet tells the king a story about two men, one rich and one poor. The poor man had one prized lamb that he treated like his own child; it would "drink from his cup, and lie in his bosom, and it was like a daughter to him." The rich man had many sheep, but when a visitor came to his house, he ordered the poor man's lamb to be taken and cooked for the feast. David, apparently believing the story to be true, cries out in anger, "As the LORD lives, the man who has done this deserves to die; he shall restore the lamb fourfold, because he did this thing, and because he had no pity" (2 Sam. 12:5–6).

There are several important things to note. The first is that David apparently did not realize he was sinning when he raped Bathsheba and had Uriah killed. That is not to excuse David, for the Bible certainly does not; rather, it demonstrates how easy it is for any of us to become complacent, so comfortable in our circumstances and with our authority that we allow our moral compass to become misaligned. We can begin to believe that our position (or that of others in authority) grants us privileges that don't apply to other people. David had become relaxed and contented in his life as king. He had defeated his enemies, and there was no one who would challenge him. Yet when Nathan rhetorically holds the mirror up to the king, David's reaction shows just how skewed his compass really is. He understands that there is an injustice in the story, but his response is to call for the man's death or, failing that, a fourfold restitution. The law called for simple compensation, at the most a repayment of double the value (Exod. 22:9), but never capital punishment. David no longer knew right from wrong; his perspective had become warped.

Nathan calls David on his hypocrisy, reminding David of all that God had given him, all that he had squandered: "Why have you despised the word of the LORD, to do what is evil in his sight?" The judgment is unflinching, and so is David's response, "I have sinned against the LORD" (2 Sam. 12:13). The consequences of his action remain, but David's immediate repentance is why God calls him a man after his own heart (1 Sam. 13:14). David acknowledges God's authority and his own guilt. In that moment of confrontation, David does not get defensive, he does not try to justify his actions or rationalize his behavior; he simply states his confession of sin.

Confession: Honest Confrontation

Whether in our corporate or personal life, we must be willing to confront and be confronted with the sin and abuse in our lives. So much suffering in this world results directly from interpersonal behavior, from exploitation of power, position, and trust. Each of us, when we face challenges and adversity, must spend time in prayer and reflection. We must be honest with ourselves before God as we assess the source of our hardship. If it comes from our own actions, then it is important that we confront that reality and accept responsibility. If it comes from the actions of others, we need to seek the strength and wisdom to confront the source. If it comes from the actions of our society or community, we need to recognize our own role in that corporate sin and be leaders in seeking repentance and reconciliation.

When those four men laid the dynamite under the steps of the Sixteenth Street Baptist Church, they were reflecting the passions and will of much of the white community of the day. They likely attended a Christian church themselves, and yet they were so committed to an ideology of racial superiority and hatred for the other that they were moved to terrorism and murder. Those men would not be brought to civil justice until forty years later, yet it was a galvanizing moment for many whites in the country, and this tragic event is credited with leading to the passage of the Civil Rights Act of 1964. Yet it should not be forgotten that the perpetrators were not a group of four isolated men. They were an expression of their community, and that community needed to confront the sin of not simply those actions but the teachings and beliefs that led to them. The need to confront communal sin remains for our community.

On Wednesday, June 17, 2015, twenty-one-year-old Dylann Roof walked into the Emanuel African Methodist Episcopal Church in downtown Charleston, South Carolina, and joined the Wednesday night Bible study. The African Methodist Episcopal Church is a historically black denomination, and "Mother Emanuel" is the oldest AME church in the South. This young white man was welcomed into their weekly Bible study group. He sat with them and debated the meaning of Scripture for nearly an hour.[6] A member of a local Lutheran congregation,[7] Roof then pulled out a gun and killed nine people in the church. He later said he hoped to spark a race war.[8] For an hour, it seemed as if there was a time of unity in the worship of Jesus Christ, and then this white man who had been welcomed into their circle of prayer killed nine people simply because they were black.

Sadly, we know that this was far from an isolated incident. There are so many mass shootings in the United States that they are almost impossible to track.[9] Being a faithful Christian or in a place of worship is no protection from the violence. Two years after the Mother Emanuel shooting, Devin Kelley fired over seven hundred rounds during the worship service of the First Baptist Church in Sutherland Springs, Texas, killing twenty-six people. These people were not killed because of their religious conviction, ethnicity, or political views. Kelley simply had had an argument with his mother-in-law, and we live in a society where such violence seemed to him to be a reasonable response.

This violence has become so routine that our country has settled into certain rhetorical patterns after such shootings. The response is immediate and predictable. There are those who call for limiting access to guns, while others insist that would be a violation of the Second Amendment of the U.S. Constitution. Everyone asks why. The pundits observe from a distance, suggesting that it is a result of the "gun culture" in the United States, that these men (and it is always men) are suffering from mental health issues, that it is the fault of the current political rhetoric, the state of the economy, or the decline in America's moral standing. When we as a society experience and observe such savagery, it is vital that we take time for honest reflection to understand why and how this can happen in our community.

There is likely some truth in all of the suggestions above. The Second Amendment is enshrined in our Constitution, providing the right for citizens to own weapons, and the result is the ready access of deadly force. Anyone who wantonly kills another person is undoubtedly suffering from *some* mental health issue, be it stress, depression, or a more pathological concern. We as a society must bear some responsibility for the climate that exists in which outrage can result in mass murder. But we as the Christian community in America must do more than assess the social and political factors at play. Like David, we must not offer various excuses or justifications for the sins of our society. We must respond with confession, repentance, and the commitment to be transformed by God. That is how the tragedy of the murder of four girls preparing for worship became the passage of the Civil Rights Act. That is how suffering becomes salvation.

Prophets like Nathan are nothing more or less than people responding to God's call that we do justice, love kindness, and walk humbly before God (Mic. 6:8). We are all called to this life and are to call others to that mission and conviction. Martin Luther King Jr. was so effective in his ministry and activism precisely because he was able to direct Americans back to the foundational promises of the Constitution and, for believers, the Bible. If we confess it, we must live it.

A hard truth of grief is that we cannot change the past. The consequences of sinful action will remain, and denying our role in bringing it about or failing to confront others will only hinder the healing. From there the road is often long and laborious. It requires prayer, repentance, and often the support of a counselor, therapist, or spiritual director. But dealing with this sort of suffering begins with acknowledging the sin in our midst—our own and that of others.

When our grief stems from the harm someone else has done—a betrayal or violent act, or sheer negligence (unlike an illness or accident, inexplicable tragedies discussed in the next chapter)—it is compounded. Their sin has become our burden, our sorrow. It is not a question of justice; it is a question of the impact on our lives. We experience in our lives the consequences of their choices. The Bible is silent on the matter, but I would imagine David and Bathsheba's relationship was never strong, given its origins in David's abusive behavior and its tragic impact on Bathsheba's life and that of her loved ones. But perhaps she was far more forgiving and gracious than I. The community of Mother Emanuel has shown grace and forgiveness. Their response to the atrocious act of one man expressing a culture of hate has been to offer forgiveness, healing, and hope. It is humbling. Truly they are an expression of "God with us."

Certainly that is Jesus' teaching for us. It is for our own sake that we must forgive others who have sinned against us (whether they ask for that forgiveness or not), so that we are not further harmed by their actions, so that we can begin our own healing. "You have heard that it was said, 'An eye for an eye and a tooth for a tooth.' But I say to you, Do not resist an evildoer. But if anyone strikes you on the right cheek, turn the other also" (Matt. 5:38–39). Jesus teaches us to let the law take care of retributive justice; we must forgive and let go, for their sake and our own.

The Result of Faithfulness

Jesus' teaching and much of the rest of the New Testament address another source of suffering, one that may be foreign to your own experiences of suffering and grief: persecution for following Jesus and proclaiming him as the Savior of the world. Jesus said that those who follow him "will be hated by all because of my name" (Matt. 10:22) and will be "blessed . . . when people revile you and persecute you and utter all kinds of evil against you falsely on my account" (Matt. 5:11). Paul famously encouraged the community of the faithful to endure suffering for Christ because "suffering produces endurance, and endurance produces character, and character produces hope, and hope does not disappoint us, because God's love has been poured into our hearts through the Holy Spirit that has been given to us" (Rom. 5:3–5). These are strong and powerful words of exhortation to a fledgling community, encouraging its members to remain firm in their new faith, even as they face the inevitable challenges and potential martyrdom.

For the early Christians, this was a very real prospect. As Jesus promised, many were rejected by their families and communities. Church tradition says that most of the disciples were martyrs, dying cruel deaths rather than renounce their belief in Jesus. There are many Christians in the world today who continue to face such persecution.

Recent news reports from the West African country of Burkina Faso tell of six people, including a priest, being murdered while they celebrated mass and of the church being burned down around them. On Easter Sunday 2019, a massive attack was launched against churches in Sri Lanka that took the lives of more than 250 worshipers and injured more than 500. A report commissioned by the United Kingdom's foreign secretary Jeremy Hunt says that global persecution of Christians has reached "genocidal levels."[10] The United Nations defines *genocide* as violence targeted against a group that is "calculated to bring about its physical destruction in whole or in part."[11] In other words, Christians in certain parts of the world are being persecuted, attacked, driven out, killed, and harassed with the purpose of removing their community from the region entirely.

For these communities, like the early church, passages such as Romans 8:31–39 offer great encouragement and sustenance in their distress: "Who will separate us from the love of Christ? Will hardship, or distress, or persecution, or famine, or nakedness, or peril, or sword? . . . [Nothing] will be able to separate us from the love of God in Christ Jesus our Lord." These communities may read the stories in the book of Daniel and see Daniel and his friends

Hananiah, Mishael, and Azariah as exemplars for the faithful in the face of martyrdom. Christ's own suffering and resurrection offers them the assurance of their faith: "For if we have been united with him in a death like his, we will certainly be united with him in a resurrection like his" (Rom. 6:5). People in such communities are facing not just the possible end of their own lives, but the end of their communities. It can seem like the end of the world. So the apocalyptic and encouraging examples from Daniel and Revelation may bring them strength and courage to persevere, to know that this world is not all that there is and that resurrection and everlasting life in Jesus is their reward.

For those of us who live in North America and Europe, such persecution is thankfully far removed. Yet when I was a young boy, I did not know what great privilege of freedom I enjoyed. I read the stories of Daniel and the warnings of Jesus, heard about the martyrs of the faith and wondered if I would ever be called upon to stand for my Savior. Would I be able to sacrifice myself for my Jesus? I read about Stephen being stoned to death while Saul held the cloaks of the executioners, and I read about St. Sebastian shot full of arrows while tied to a tree. In church I heard about modern martyrs who delivered Bibles behind the Iron Curtain and were never heard from again. I even have a vivid memory of being told about a prisoner of war in Vietnam who kept his mind focused and his spirit strong by writing down on the walls of his cell Scripture verses he had memorized. I was stricken; I could barely remember the Twenty-third Psalm. To this day, I have a horrible memory for recitation. How would I ever be counted among the faithful? I am not being flippant or funny; this caused me great concern and anxiety.

At some point I began to realize that unless I willingly took myself out into those parts of the world where Christians were persecuted, there was very little chance that I would be called upon to give up my life for my faith. Those of you living in the United States are unlikely to have faced anything like persecution for your Christian faith and won't, unless you intentionally place yourself into such a situation. It is true that you may have been mocked for your faith and you might even have been challenged at work or even turned down for a job. But mockery is not martyrdom, and prejudice is not persecution.

In my career, I have had to be very careful to be open and honest about my faith, since being a scholar of rabbinic Judaism with a name like "Christian" does tend to raise questions. "What's a nice Jewish boy like you doing with a name like 'Christian'?" was the most commonly asked question I received in my six years as director of Jewish studies at Tulane University. In fact, before I got that position, I was told that I should go by "Chris" rather than "Christian" if I wanted a job in the field. (In point of fact, I was named after an uncle. As devout as my parents were, they were not making a statement of faith in naming me.) Most thought it was a wonderful oddity and a sign of the academic integrity of the program, but there were many students and community members who made it clear that they thought it odd at best and disgraceful at worst that I was the director.

In another instance at another university, I was hosting a dinner for a distinguished guest lecturer, a Nobel Prize winner no less, whom our committee had invited to speak as part of a series on science and religion. This guest was a self-described Jewish atheist and had spoken about the way in which science can explain many phenomena heretofore explained by religion. He himself was very magnanimous about the role of faithful people in academia, but as we discussed other potential speakers, one of our dinner party objected to my suggestion of a prominent geneticist who was also known as an evangelical Christian. This other dinner guest opined, "No one who believes in God should be allowed on the faculty in a respectable university." Sitting across from him, I raised an eyebrow and said something to the effect of, "Is that right?" To which he replied, "Yes, and I don't think you should be here either." I was the host of the dinner, the dean of the college, and yet I was being publicly called out for my faith. But I would hardly call that persecution. Persecution of a person or group requires prejudice *and* power *and* persistent oppression. Christians in the United States of America are not a persecuted group.

To be clear, I am a white man from a middle-class family with all sorts of benefits and privileges. Many in our country *do* regularly experience prejudice based on their race, ethnicity, sexual orientation, and religion that is harmful, degrading, demeaning, and devastating. My experiences cannot be compared to theirs. The power structure, prejudicial treatment against them, and the consistent nature of that treatment means that there are people in the United States who can rightly claim to be persecuted. In the time I have been writing this book, there have been mass shootings by white men in black churches and synagogues—in our country. While our Muslim and Jewish compatriots are targeted because of their religion, those in Mother Emanuel were targeted because of their race, not their religion.

In spite of the reality that in America Christians are not persecuted for their faith and that often those who are committing heinous crimes do so while claiming to follow Jesus, we continue to hear in the news and from pulpits across this country that American Christians are being persecuted. We are told there is a "war on Christmas," and opinion pieces are written asking, "How long will I be allowed to remain a Christian?" Those who call themselves "Christians" may indeed be challenged for their beliefs, and the time of Christianity as the dominant culture in the United States may well be fading, but to assert that Christianity is under attack in America is an exaggeration, if not completely false, and is spiritually harmful.

There is little doubt that there will be moments in life when we as confessing Christians will face prejudice, even in the United States. It should not surprise us that having the Gospel priorities of valuing the poorest among us, seeking to ensure justice for those who are outside of society, and providing food, shelter, and clothing for those in need will be in conflict with a culture of prioritizing our own needs and comforts over those of others. It is in the Sermon on the Mount where Jesus promises that those who follow him will be reviled and persecuted (Matt. 5). It is the same sermon in which he encourages and challenges his followers to be humble and meek, to seek out righteousness and mercy, to be peacemakers. When we are doing those things, we will find ourselves at odds with the priorities of the world, and we will be attacked, sometimes from within our own churches and communities. In those times, we should rightly cling to the promise Jesus made: "Blessed are those who are persecuted for righteousness' sake, for theirs is the kingdom of heaven" (Matt. 5:10).

Paul echoes Jesus' message when he writes, "Do not be conformed to this world, but be transformed by the renewing of your minds, so that you may discern what is the will of God—what is good and acceptable and perfect" (Rom. 12:2). Living the Gospel life will, of necessity, mean that we are behaving counter to the way of "this world." When you "bless those who persecute you," "associate with the lowly," "do not claim to be wiser than you are," and "do not repay anyone evil for evil" (Rom. 12:14–17), you will stand apart from the rest of the world; that will garner ridicule, if nothing else. When we find ourselves suffering for these reasons, when our simple confession of faith, our love for the unlovely, and our humility causes others to mock, shame, and revile us, then we "are sharing Christ's sufferings, so that [we] may also be glad and shout for joy when his glory is revealed" (1 Pet. 4:13).

This is the heart of the New Testament teaching on suffering for and because of our faith in Christ. Unlike hardship that comes as a consequence of sin or "the remainder" that arrives in our lives simply because we live in this broken world, suffering for living out our faith is a blessed burden that comes from doing what is holy and right. There is nothing easy about rejection, even for those living in a country like the United States; in many places in our world, following Christ might well lead to death. Yet if we are reviled and persecuted for Christ, then we are blessed by the Spirit of God. "Therefore, let those suffering in accordance with God's will entrust themselves to a faithful Creator, while continuing to do good" (1 Pet. 4:19).

We experience life as a complicated combination of suffering and grace, yet we seem to expect the grace and question the suffering. The latter is understandable and spiritually healthy, even as we remind ourselves of Wolterstorff's warning that "to the 'why' of suffering we get no firm answer." Scripture provides some insight, offering both the examples of lives lived and laws to be followed, but in all contexts, it is intended to encourage, to provide us with guidance and hope to enable us to move forward in grace and peace even, and especially, when we don't know the "why."

Creator and Redeemer whose property it is always to have mercy, pour out your Spirit upon us, be present with us, and grant us your peace as we bring before you in prayer our pain, our grief, and our questions. For in you we live and move and have our being, now and forever. Amen.

Reflection Questions

1. Do you struggle to identify the cause of your suffering, or is it relatively clear? Do you struggle with the "what ifs" of assigning blame to yourself and others?
2. Where have you seen the consequences of sin in your life, whether it is your own sin or that committed by

others? How do you respond when you feel wronged by the sins of others?

3. What examples of communal sin come first to your mind? When you find that you are part of a society that is doing harm to others, how do you feel? How do you respond to people who have been harmed by the community's sin?

4. Have you ever felt like you were suffering because of your faithfulness? How was that circumstance similar to and different from the persecution experienced by biblical martyrs and Christians in other countries today?

5. How does the Bible help you make sense of loss and suffering? Do you identify with the struggles of any biblical characters in particular?

CHAPTER 4

THE REMAINDER

One of my earliest memories is from my fifth summer. I was learning how to swim, and I had been entered in my first swim meet; it was a Wednesday or a Thursday night at some other pool. It was very dark, especially in the water, and I had never yet swum a full length of the twenty-five-meter pool. My father promised me a trip to Toys "R" Us (of blessed memory) if I swam the whole length without stopping to grab onto the ropes. Not only did I do that, but I took only one breath and was so quick that later in the week I was moved up to the "A" team to swim on Saturday mornings. I went on to be a very good swimmer, earning full scholarship offers to several very good universities and swimming programs. But what I remember most about that night was heading to the hospital after the stop at Toys "R" Us and playing with my newly purchased cars on the blue carpeted floor of the waiting room.

"Your mom may die," someone said. I don't know who told me that, but it was one of the first truths I learned. Of course, we all will die, but as a young child I already knew that my mom's illness might take her life. In my mind, I connect that knowledge with those cheap tin cars on that blue carpet after that swim meet. I don't recall crying or being sad, just accepting that this was our life. I did not yet know what other people's lives or families were like. Ours involved going to the hospital and the doctor's—a lot.

By the time I was in junior high, I could tell you that my mom had systemic lupus erythematosus. Lupus.org explains that it "is a chronic autoimmune disease that can damage any part of the body (skin, joints, and/or organs). 'Chronic' means that the signs and symptoms tend to last longer than six weeks and often for many years." In my mom's case, it has lasted from her diagnosis in early 1961 until now; she is currently in her eighty-third year, and scientists have still not found a cure for lupus.

Going to the clinics was as much a part of our lives as going to church. Every Sunday we had a thirty-minute drive to church, and so that the time would not be wasted, Dad would have a sermon from J. Vernon McGee on the radio as we drove to church. Once there, we had Sunday school, and then the entire family sat together in the pews for one of Dr. Halverson's Bible-centered sermons. Often we would return to church for the Sunday evening service, meaning it was not uncommon that we would hear three sermons on any given Sunday. Today I call Dr. Halverson's method of preaching "expository," but as a child I simply knew that his sermons were long. This Bible-focused teaching of my childhood, even from my earliest days, provided me with the context in which I would understand my mom's poor health.

As I grew and understood more about God and Jesus, this world we live in, and my mom's health, I saw that my mom was suffering in a way that was unjust, or at least undeserved. She had not sinned in any way that might have warranted divine punishment. She had not taken this illness upon herself as her father had unwittingly done (along with tens of thousands of people) by smoking packs of Lucky Strike cigarettes every day from the age of fourteen. She was not being persecuted for her faith. My mom had a disease. I learned early on that things like that happen.

They happen because we live in a broken world where what had been created perfect and good is now distorted and sick. It was not sin or society that caused my mom's illness or my son's blood infection; it is simply the nature of this world. We want to understand why these things happen, but as with so much suffering in life, "It is what it is" is the only explanation we are afforded. As Nicholas Wolterstorff says, "The meaning of the remainder is not told us. It eludes us. Our net of meaning is too small."[1] While the meaning of the remainder may elude us, the Bible nonetheless contains a number of reflections on this most common of life experiences. After all, as the author of Ecclesiastes observes, "there is nothing new under the sun" (Eccl. 1:9).

We have already touched upon the fact that Ecclesiastes and Job are probably the best-known biblical meditations on the inscrutable nature of suffering. Job is the book most read and preached in Christian circles, with the main figure often praised for his patience and perseverance. Yet too often we ignore the central fact of this story: Job and his family have done nothing to deserve the devastation that befalls them.

We Don't Know

Tragedy occurs all the time, without notice and without justification. As I was writing this very section of this book, I received a text message from a close friend whose son had been on Mack's soccer team, the State College Celtics: "We need to talk ASAP. Another tragedy in Celtic family." The sister of one of their teammates had died in an equestrian accident. Ashley was a junior national champion doing a routine jump she and her horse had done hundreds, if not thousands, of times before, and the horse tumbled and fell on top of her. There is no reason, no justification for this life taking. It was a tragic accident that has left a family and a community grieving and asking again the simple question, "Why?"

Ashley's grandfather went to the justice of the matter. "I am a faithful man, but I cannot understand how God could leave so many scumbags alive and yet take this beautiful, innocent girl." His priest responded simply, "There is no answer." As we stood in the funeral home parlor, with family and friends all around and Ashley's beautiful and obscene casket on one side of the room, he told me, "That was the answer I needed. I expected him to give me some sort of BS about God's inscrutable will, plan, or some such nonsense. But he answered it straight, 'We don't know.'" There is comfort in that answer; there is reassurance in such humility.

We want meaning, we want purpose, and yet so often "our net of meaning is too small"; we simply have no answer to the question. And can there ever really be a satisfying answer? What explanation could possibly be offered for Mack's or Ashley's death that would satisfy us? Would Job have been satisfied with the explanation for why his children were taken? When comparing their lives with the book of Job, many seek to find comfort in the preface, which provides some explanation for Job's suffering. They assure themselves and others that, like Job, God is controlling and has designed every event and experience in their life. I want to pause and be clear: if that brings you comfort and solace, then please, accept that teaching and live in that grace.

For many of us, however, such an explanation is not satisfactory, and such a reading of Job ignores the main point and purpose of the book: *Job never knows why his family and he suffered.* Yes, the audience knows the preface, but consider the story from Job's perspective. Job was living in the midst of pain and anguish, and there was no answer his friends could provide that could accommodate his loss. That is where Ashley's parents and brother find themselves. Any of us who have lost children will tell you the same. The strength of the book of Job is found not in the framing preface and conclusion, but in the fact that Job is living in a world that many of us know all too well, where there is no satisfactory answer for our suffering.

Job and his wife simply experience their life and loss as it crashes into their lives, much as we do. We would be remiss if we did not remember that Job's wife loses as much as Job, even if she does not suffer within her own body. We do not hear her voice except in one famous statement: "Do you still persist in your integrity? Curse God, and die!" (Job 2:9). This comment is invoked in various contexts, often in jest, yet she articulates the core thesis of the book of Job. How do we respond to catastrophe? Do we accept it silently, meekly, accepting whatever comes upon us in faith (or ignorance)? Do we assume that we have done something wrong to deserve such punishment and spend our lives in close introspection of our actions and motives and unresolved guilt? Do we curse God? Do we just give up and die? Or is there some *via media*, some middle road, that can be followed, as winding and painful as it may be? In the end, the book itself offers no firm resolution to any of these issues but rather serves as what James Crenshaw calls a "paradigm of an unanswered lament, a model for those undergoing present suffering."[2] Job answers his wife by persisting in his integrity *and* challenging God.

Job the book and the figure himself offer us the example of living through unexplained hardship with a faith and commitment to God *and* a refusal to accept easy answers or false security. It is an ultimate statement of faith to acknowledge the power and authority of God and say, "Therefore I will not restrain my mouth; I will speak in the anguish of my spirit; I will complain in the bitterness of my soul" (Job 7:11). After our son died, I wrote extensively on my blog about our loss, my feelings, my reflections on the theology of it all. People thanked me for it, saying that it was "brave" of me to share so openly. I honestly do not know if I could have done otherwise. It was my lament; whether anyone read it was irrelevant. I needed to get all those thoughts and feelings out of me, and the blog was my outlet. I am humbled and truly thankful that so many found my mutterings helpful, but I was only following Job's example, speaking in the anguish of my spirit, unwilling to accept an easy answer and trying to be honest with myself and God.

Not Helpful

It is ironic that Job is often the place where verses are mined for nuggets of wisdom that seem to advocate a humble and contrite response to adversity. The intent is to encourage. Yet the effort often fails because the context is ignored and the statement being shared as an affirmation of faith is, in fact, from the mouth of one of Job's friends and as such is a premise being challenged by the author, not one held up for emulation. For example, consider the "comforting" words of Eliphaz at the beginning of Job's suffering:

How happy is the one whom God reproves;
   therefore do not despise the discipline of the Almighty.
For he wounds, but he binds up;
   he strikes, but his hands heal.
He will deliver you from six troubles;
   in seven no harm shall touch you.

—Job 5:17–19

Such statements as Eliphaz's are certainly in keeping with what can be found in Proverbs, and it aligns with passages such as Deuteronomy 28, but they presuppose that the one being disciplined has done something to deserve God's reproof. Job knows that he has feared and worshiped God and that there is no reason for such disciplinary action in his life. Yet his friend is convinced that Job's self-assessment is wrong and offers as proof the fact that

Eliphaz has never seen the innocent or the upright suffer affliction without cause:

> Think now, who that was innocent ever perished?
> Or where were the upright cut off?
> As I have seen, those who plow iniquity
> and sow trouble reap the same.
> —Job 4:7–8

In Eliphaz's view, and that of much of biblical theology, the very fact that Job is experiencing such incredible suffering and hardship is evidence that he has done *something* wrong. How could it be otherwise? Yet that is the very premise of the book of Job—to challenge the received teaching, to complicate the worldview by acknowledging and addressing the fact that the innocent do suffer, and often. It is a fact of life that unmerited suffering occurs; when it does, the standard theological explanation that it is due to God's discipline or to persecution for one's faith is not adequate, nor are the correlated encouragements.

Job pushes back against his friends and God, maintaining his innocence. In fairness to Job's friends, from their perspective, Job simply seems to be arrogant, insisting that there can be nothing he has done to warrant such treatment. Who hasn't done wrong in their life? The lesson from Job is not that we are to stand arrogantly in our righteous indignation and insist on our innocence. When there can be no justification of our suffering, then it is right to express to God our complaint, to lament our plight and insist that God look and see how we suffer.

The real difficulty of the friends' remarks is that they are neither wrong nor right. In some circumstances their comments would be exactly right. Arrogant people who will not acknowledge their own hubris and sin should be challenged (Matt. 18) and encouraged to repent. We ought to maintain a humble posture and learn from those who have gone before (Job 8:8–10). But terrible things happen in life, and there is so much suffering that occurs in this world that does not align with either discipline or discipleship. In such cases, what was meant as encouragement and support becomes salt rubbed into open and painful sores.

Discernment is what is needed. We have to think, prayerfully and carefully, about our lives and the lives of those we wish to support. Our lives are a complex combination of circumstances, and we must acknowledge that. It would be far easier if there was always a simple one-to-one correspondence and explanation for why some succeed and others fail, why some flourish and others are riddled with disease, why some are blessed and others cursed. Then we would always know the right thing to say and do; we could just look it up in a manual. Sadly, that is how many treat the Bible, and in so doing they either misapply its teachings or, finding it wanting (when it is really their method of reading and application that is at fault), determine that the Bible is unrealistic at best and untrue at worst. We are often no better than Job's friends, offering platitudes and explanations for trauma and pain that are unexplainable and unjustifiable.

Ironically, if we are looking for a biblical model of how to care for those in mourning, the best example is Job's friends. It is not what they said, but what they did (Job 2:11–13). First, they determined to go and be with Job in his distress. Then they came and grieved with him; they too were moved, and they wept. And then they were silent: "They sat with him on the ground seven days and seven nights, and no one spoke a word to him, for they saw that his suffering was very great." To be silent is perhaps the hardest thing for some of us to learn. Yet what people most need in their distress is to know that they are not alone, to know that they are loved and remembered, and to know that others feel their grief as well.

Ecclesiastes offers a similar message: "It is better to go to the house of mourning than to go to the house of feasting; for this is the end of everyone, and the living will lay it to heart" (Eccl. 7:2). It is a seemingly fatalistic view ("for this is the end of everyone"), yet it is remarkably encouraging and practical advice for caring for those who mourn. You go to a party, you might have fun, but will people really care that you were there? If you go to a funeral, if you call up a friend whose husband, wife, father, friend, or child has died and you just be with them, they will remember. Our family and Ashley's family may not remember exactly who was among the hundreds who came to our children's funerals, but we *know* you were there. Go, be present in the house of mourning. The living, those who remain behind and are missing those who have gone ahead, will feel that in their heart. And we will be grateful.

It Is Enough

The truth that Ecclesiastes and Job present to us and the encouragement they offer is that we often simply don't know, and that is and can be enough. Ultimately, we do not have all the answers. Whether you take the view that *everything* is orchestrated by God or that God remains sovereign and yet allows humanity and the world to move in its own way, all of us admit that we do not and cannot know for sure why certain tragedies occur. They just do. We want to know why. We think we need to know why in order to move on, in order to make sense of it all, to put order into our lives and find a purpose and a place for our tragedy. But this world simply "is what it is," and that means that whatever purpose there may be behind an event or action, much is unknowable. In the next two chapters we will consider ways in which we can *create meaning* out of our tragedies, ways in which we can have purpose in our progress through grief, but we cannot leave this chapter without considering what answer God did provide to Job.

Maintaining his innocence and pushing back against his friends, Job continues to demand a reply from God, an explanation of the reason for his grief and suffering.

(This is, in fact, one key distinction between Job's complaint and that of most psalms of lament. Job wants to know why, what purpose there might be to his family's calamity. In most laments it is enough to simply declare, "Look, God, and see what you have done to me!") Finally, in chapter 38, God speaks to Job; God answers his call, yet God never answers his questions. In fact, God begins by questioning Job:

"Who is this that darkens counsel by words without
   knowledge?
Gird up your loins like a man,
   I will question you, and you shall declare to me.
Where were you when I laid the foundation of the earth?
   Tell me, if you have understanding."
   —Job 38:2–4

Of course, Job (like ourselves) does not have understanding, and that is the whole point!

God's answer to Job seems decidedly lacking in content and comfort. God basically says to Job, repeatedly and loudly, are you God? Or even *a god*? Because if you could raise up and sustain the heavens and the earth, if you could tame Leviathan and best Behemoth, then you would understand, then we could have a conversation. There is so much about this world that is unknown and unknowable, from knowing when the mountain goats give birth and how the hawk soars to having seen the gates of death—there is so much that you do not know, says God.

When I read these passages today, I think to myself, "But there *are* people who know when the mountain goat gives birth and who have comprehended and measured the expanse of the earth." And that is part of the problem. We think we *can* know everything; given enough time and ingenuity, we think we can mark, measure, and explain everything in life. It is this desire to control the whirlwind that leads to theologies of predestination and sovereignty that reduce all of creation and human experience to a clockwork mechanism. But we also need humility; we need to acknowledge that there are simply some things we will not and cannot know. The impulse and the desire to put all things in order and to know all things is real, human, and understandable. After all, it emerges from being created in the image of God. We are inquisitive and creative beings made in God's image, but we are not God. And when God speaks to Job out of the whirlwind, he reminds him of that fact. Somehow, Job seems satisfied.

God has spoken, and Job is humbled:

I know that you can do all things,
  and that no purpose of yours can be thwarted.
. . . .
Therefore, I have uttered what I did not understand,
  things too wonderful for me, which I did not know.
. . . .
I had heard of you by the hearing of the ear,
  but now my eye sees you;
therefore, I despise myself,
  and repent in dust and ashes."
                                            — Job 42:2–6

Job is humbled, yet he is not defeated. Whereas most English translations, as the New Revised Standard Version here, render that final passage as Job saying, "I despise myself," it is better translated as something like "I withdraw my argument." That makes for poor poetry in English, so the Jewish Publication Society version has "therefore, I recant and relent."[3] God has responded to Job, and in light of God's self-revelation and the awareness of his own limitations, Job recants his position. He does not admit any guilt that might justify the treatment of himself or his family, and God does not indict him of any such sins, but Job acknowledges that God has spoken.

God has spoken. That is why Job accepts the fact that God did not answer his questions, because God has spoken to him: "I had heard of you by the hearing of the ear, but now my eye sees you." What Job had known by intellect and teaching, the sort of wisdom that his friends provided in their efforts to get him to repent of his sins, was inadequate. But now Job has experienced God, and that has changed everything.

The message of Job is not a typical message of comfort and consolation. It certainly is not the sort of comfort and consolation that *we* want, that we think we need. There is no answer, no explanation, at least from Job's perspective, for why his children were killed, his wealth and property destroyed, and his own body ruined. Yet there is the experience of God speaking to him. Many are the days, the minutes, when *all I wish for is to hear God speak to me*. I have knowledge and learning, but I want my eye to see God, to experience God. I think, I hope, that would be enough.

The message of Job is not the typical message of comfort and consolation. It should, however, be empowering to those of us who ask of God "Why?" and "How could you?" Like the Teacher in Ecclesiastes, Job seeks purpose and meaning and is unwilling to accept a pat answer that does not fit his own, real, lived experience. The world, and our experience in it, is complicated, messy, and painful. The Bible provides guidance and direction and is sufficient for us. The Bible also reminds us through Job and Ecclesiastes that there is much that is beyond our knowledge and understanding. So we must open up our hearts and throats, calling out to God in lamentation and complaint, honestly laying bare our pain and grief. Then, out of the whirlwind, out of the tumult of hospitals and tears, funerals and sleepless nights, God will speak, and we will listen.

O God, by whom the meek are guided in judgment, and light rises
up in darkness for the godly: Grant us, in all our doubts and
uncertainties, the grace to ask what you would have us do, that
the Spirit of wisdom may save us from all false choices, and that
in your light we may see light, and in your straight path may not
stumble; through Jesus Christ our Lord. Amen.[4]

Reflection Questions

1. Reflect on your childhood and early life. When did you first realize that suffering was a common, and often inexplicable, part of life in the world?
2. Do you find it easier to cope with tragedies that have a clear cause or those that seem to "just happen"? How do you respond differently to suffering in those categories?
3. Does the knowledge that you did nothing to deserve the suffering you experience comfort you or anger you?
4. What can others say or do that is helpful in processing your grief? What words or actions are unhelpful or even hurtful?
5. How does it affect you to know that God sees and acknowledges your pain? If God would speak audibly to you right now, what would you want to hear?

CHAPTER 5

ONE STEP

On January 18, 2013, just two weeks after Mack died, I posted a short reflection on my blog. Mourning, I wrote, is a bit like being forced to wear a pair of painful, ill-fitting shoes. They hurt like hell and make you limp, wince, and cry, but you can't take them off. The only way to ease the pain is to start walking, to break them in. Blisters form, then calluses, and then the limp begins to settle in. After a while, months or years (I still don't know when), I imagine that you begin to think less and less about what shoes you are wearing, and most people won't notice the limp and the occasional wince. In the meantime, it just hurts.

I am the first to admit that it is not a perfect analogy, but I continue to expand upon it. Imagine that those shoes, as ill-fitting as they are, look *great*. Other people may never know that those shoes cause me deep pain, that I am only able to walk about through the day because of continued effort that allows the calluses to form protective barriers, that each step requires such a force of will that I never needed before I put on those shoes. What they may see, if I am coping, is a well-dressed person headed to work, going about his day. The shoes look fine, nice even, and my stride may halt or falter a bit, but it's nothing too out of the ordinary, just someone living life as usual. When we suffer deep loss, nothing is "usual" anymore.

C. S. Lewis is well known for his analogies, and while I believe I had read *A Grief Observed* when I was younger, I do not know if his foot-related comparison was in my mind in those weeks after Mack's death or not. Many people have reminded me of it:

> To say the patient is getting over it after an operation for appendicitis is one thing; after he's had his leg off is quite another. After that operation either the wounded stump heals or the man dies. If it heals, the fierce, continuous pain will stop. Presently he'll get back his strength and be able to stump about on his wooden leg. He has "got over it." But he will probably have recurrent pains in the stump all his life, and perhaps pretty bad ones; and he will always be a one-legged man. There will be hardly any moment when he forgets it. Bathing, dressing, sitting down and getting up again, even lying in bed, will all be different. His whole way of life will be changed. All sorts of pleasures and activities that he once took for granted will have to be simply written off. Duties too. At present I am learning to get about on crutches. Perhaps I shall presently be given a wooden leg. But I shall never be a biped again.[1]

This too is an apt analogy. We who have lost a loved one, especially one as close as a spouse or child, have lost a critical part of our being. We are no longer whole. I do think the analogy falls down a bit, since people usually notice when someone has a prosthetic limb. Most people do not know when we are grieving or suffering. When Lewis was writing, he and his society had come through two world wars. Many men in Britain made their way painfully along the streets and lanes maimed and scarred, physically and emotionally, from those battles. The nation understood that and often showed respect and gratitude to these warriors. Sadly, today many of our veterans again move about our communities on crutches, in wheelchairs, and with artificial limbs. The legs are no longer wooden and offer a greater amount of mobility and comfort to the injured, but they live with the reality that they shall never be whole again. People in the street can see their injury; they take notice and perhaps will offer support or sympathy or gratitude for their service. People who are grieving have no such external wounds, no indicators of the battles they have endured.

When our son died, my mom reflected upon something her doctor had told her when my grandfather died. Mom was grieving deeply for her father, and the doctor commented that it was a shame we no longer wear black armbands as people did in the past. Then, at least, people would know that we were mourning, that our life was not, at this moment, what it had been before. When my father died, my sister-in-law, Jenni, made a black wreath with a yellow rose (my father was very proud of his Texas heritage) and placed it on the door of my parents' home. Mom had suggested this as a way of letting the neighbors know that Dad had died without having to speak to each one, something she just wasn't quite ready for. It was a great solution to that painful problem and had the added benefit of providing Jenni with a way to show her love and act in her grief.

These are the outward marks of the trauma we bear. But what about the wounds that never appear on the flesh? Anyone who enters and survives battle leaves changed, altered internally if not externally. The truth is that we *all* have seen battles, we all carry our wounds. Some of us are graced with a time of, well, grace—a few years or perhaps even decades when our conflicts and struggles are not more than puberty and a few personal rejections. But most of us carry deep hurts. Most people in this world, even in such an affluent country as the United States, experience hunger, poverty, prejudice, and losses that wound and maim. And once that happens to us, we never will be the same.

In those moments we can feel isolated and alone. The truth is that the grief and pain that we each feel at the loss of something is unique; it is our own. As much as those around us offer their love and support (and even their silent presence can bring strength and comfort), we each walk our own path through this valley.

Mack was a well-loved boy, not just within our immediate and extended family, but in the community. Each of us missed him in different ways; we each grieved in different ways. His buddies on his soccer team missed their goalkeeper who kept them in close games and whose skill won them more than a few. They missed their silly friend who made them laugh. And likely for the first time in their lives they were realizing that this life comes with loss. Each had his own relationship with Mack and his own, unique trauma he was trying to cope with—at the age of eight. These friends were surrounded by people who loved them and Mack, but each had to take that perilous, interior journey on his own. Many rallied around them to provide comfort and crutchlike support, and I am so thankful to say that they are growing strong and well, but they and God alone know the depth of their sorrow.

It was true as well even for those of us closest to Mack. As his parents, Elizabeth and I obviously felt this enormous void, yet that hole in each of our lives was not the same. Elizabeth looks at images of Mary and the child Jesus and remembers holding her little boy. She takes strength from reflecting on Mary's loss and remembers the moments that only a mother has with her child. I pick up and reassemble the LEGO bricks that Mack and I put together and remember the silly joys we shared. Those LEGOs are sacred, no less holy to me than the chalice we use in the Eucharist. Neither of us grieves more or less than the other; we grieve together, each in our own space of pain and memory, a morbid version of the "parallel play" that children engage in when young. We grieve in our own way, but we grieve *together*.

How do we walk on, through this world with our accumulated scratches and scars? How do we lace up those painful shoes or put on that prosthetic leg each morning? How do we carry on, day after day? That continues to be one of the most commonly asked questions we receive. When we were at the funeral for Ashley, the sister of one of Mack's buddies, so many of those people who were there had been at Mack's funeral. Here we all were again. The community, this time extended to include the equestrian world, had again come together to love and support a family in disbelief and grief. We all were grieving together, with them. Ashley's parents, our friends, everyone asked, "How do you do it? How can you carry on?" We hugged them, held them, and said, "By grace." And because we have no choice. We must carry on, we must continue to live and love for one another, for our daughter, and for Mack. And we do so in, through, and with the grace that is offered to us: the presence of God.

Gracious Grief

When Adam and Eve had chosen to forge their own path, a path that led away from God, they were confronted with their disobedience and the consequences of their decision. God punished them, and yet he does not abandon them. God provides for them: "And the LORD God made garments of skins for the man and for his wife, and clothed them" (Gen. 3:21). There, in the midst of their new self-awareness of nakedness and shame of sin, and overwhelmed with the realization that their whole world is never to be the same, they are graciously provided with warmth and protection. Granted, compared with what they have just lost it is not much, but it is comfort, and it enables them to take their next steps.

It is a small passage, one verse before we move on to what many see as another act of grace—removing humanity from the garden so that they may not eat of the tree of life and live forever with their new, painful knowledge. Yet it serves as a reminder that in our own time of grief God remains with us, offering us comfort if we will accept it. We may no longer walk in the garden with God, but evidence of the divine love and care for us remains.

When we are in those times of grief and loss, in the midst of our own frustration and hurt, we find that there is often someone offering us some seemingly small kindness. In the face of the loss of a child, a chicken casserole can seem absurd (for the one giving and the one receiving), and yet it is grace. That simple offering removes from us the need to think about groceries, cooking, and the day-to-day duties that we must eventually get back to but in mourning are simply too much to consider. It also shows the other person's love for us and allows them to participate in our grief as well. It is also just for a time. (However, we found a green bean casserole, the kind with the dried onions on top, in our basement freezer three years after Mack had died. Some things last longer than others.) We who grieve should be willing to accept these small acts when they come, not only for ourselves but for the blessing of the giver as well. That chicken casserole is a holy gift. Remember, the offering in the Communion service is not the money collected; it is the bread and wine brought forward by members of the congregation to place upon the Lord's Table—small, simple, basic fare, but the sacramental substance of eternal life.

When God made those clothes for the man and woman, they were just some basic clothes, hardly anything in comparison to what they had just lost, had just given away. Yet those clothes were sacramental. According to *The Book of Common Prayer*, "Sacraments are outward and visible signs of inward and spiritual grace."[2] Those clothes of skin were not simply to provide protection and physical comfort, but were also symbols, reminders of God's continued presence with the man and the woman as they left the safety of the garden.

Seeing and receiving these elements of grace is the hard work of living in a broken world. I remember well the first time I saw that inspirational poster with an image of footprints in the sand. I was in college, and a friend in our Christian fellowship had it on her wall. There is a lovely picture of a sandy beach with two sets of footprints walking along, just above the surf, and then there is only one set. The text on the poster usually says something like, "Lord, you promised to always be with me, but in the most troubling times of my life, I only see one set of footprints." The Lord responds, "My child, I will never leave you. When you saw only one set of footprints, that was when I carried you."[3]

It is a lovely image, and of course it follows the well-worn metaphor of our life as a journey with God as our companion. Yet it obfuscates the reality and nature of the path we walk upon. The shore is often hard and rocky; footprints, if they can be seen, will always include our own as well. God does not leave us, but we still must make the passage with our feet on the ground. And then there are all the other pilgrims who are alongside us as well. Our struggles and sorrows may be our own, yet we are not alone.

This companionship is a blessing, but it is sometimes, well, perhaps not a curse, but hardly encouraging. Job confronts God and demands an accounting of all his suffering and loss: "Today also my complaint is bitter; his hand is heavy despite my groaning. *Oh, that I knew where I might find him*, that I might come even to his dwelling!" (Job 23:2–3, emphasis mine). Like the person addressing God in the footprints poem, Job wants to know where God is as he is enduring this unjustifiable hardship. This is Job's plight, even among his friends and wife. He feels abandoned by all, including God. "Oh, that I knew where I might find him!"

We do *not* walk alone, nor is our divine companion lacking in compassion. Yet it remains for us to accept his presence with us. "Let us therefore approach the throne of grace with boldness, so that we may receive mercy and find grace to help in time of need" (Heb. 4:16). When the inevitable tragedy strikes, we may feel powerless and a victim and, in that moment, we may well be both. Yet we still have agency, the ability to make decisions for ourselves about how we will respond to the tragedy, what path we will take from that moment of trauma. A first step is toward God. The evidence of God's presence with us is there even if sometimes we have to seek it out. We might not know where to find God, but God knows where to find us, even in the darkest, deepest valleys.

Psalm 23 is probably the only psalm I was able to memorize as a kid; I have never been good at rote memorization. The traditional rendering of verse 4 is well-known: "Yea, though I walk through *the valley of the shadow of death* . . ." As I began to learn Hebrew in college, I remember my teacher and friend, Richard Wright, pointing out to me that the original wording is better translated as something like "valley of deepest darkness," which is reflected in the New Revised Standard Version: "Even though I walk through the darkest valley, I fear no evil; for you are with me; your rod and your staff—they comfort me." It might be set aside as a distinction without a difference, but as I have mulled on this over the years, I have come to appreciate the greater breadth of meaning in "the darkest valley."

"The valley of the shadow of death" had seemed something supernatural to me when I was younger, something otherworldly, like a line from Tolkien as the Fellowship of the Ring is journeying through Moria. Or, if I associated it with things of this world, I thought of being by my

grandfather's deathbed. In that setting, it was about immanent death. The depiction found in Psalm 23 is fuller and
broader than that. The LORD, our constant companion, is
leading us throughout life with all its twists and turns. The
valley is not a box canyon that is a dead-end, but a passage through which we journey without being able to see
or know where our next steps should be. And in *that* darkness God leads us.

In that respect, I suppose it is akin to Tolkien's description of the Fellowship journeying through Moria. It even
includes Gandalf's sacrificial offering of himself and his
descent into death so that the others may pass safely
through to the other side. Yet where they had orcs chasing
them, making the image otherworldly, we have the mundane fears and stumbling blocks of depression and anxiety, sickness and death, joblessness and insecurity. It is not
just in the face of immanent death that God is with us, but
throughout the entire journey. Perhaps today we might use
the image, as prosaic as it seems, of a tour guide, the one
who can lead us through an unexplored city, keeping us
safe from muggers and thieves and ensuring that, whatever
adventures we experience, at the end of the day we arrive
safe and sound at our hotel.

Is such language too commonplace to describe our relationship with God? I don't think so. The psalmist was writing out of his own real-life experience, one shared by many
shepherds throughout history as they protected and led
their flocks to food and water. That is the power of understanding that phrase as the "deepest darkness" and not just
the "shadow of death"; it is the normalcy of it, the commonplace image of being in a dark place, unsure of your
surroundings. Death is like that, at least for those of us left
behind. We suddenly find ourselves in unfamiliar terrain
with another unseen rock or boulder cropping up to take
us down at any moment. Yet day by day we also walk in
dark places, and God is with us there as well.

Present Presence (or "The Lord with You")

This biblical truth, that God is present with us even in our most extreme need, is found throughout the Bible. God *is* present, God *is* with us. Consider when God first told Moses that he had heard the prayers of his people and was sending him to bring them up out of their captivity: "But Moses said to God, 'Who am I that I should go to Pharaoh, and bring the Israelites out of Egypt?' He said, 'I will be with you; and this shall be the sign for you that it is I who sent you: when you have brought the people out of Egypt, you shall worship God on this mountain'" (Exod. 3:11–12). No doubt Moses was more than a bit nervous and scared. Leaving aside the whole burning bush thing for a moment, the prospect of taking on the Egyptians was undoubtedly a point of concern. In fact, Moses objects three times to God's calling him to this task.

But notice God's first response to him: "I will be with you." It is the same assurance that was given to Gideon when God called him to deliver his tribe from the Midianites: "The angel of the LORD appeared to him and said to him, "The LORD is with you, you mighty warrior" (Judg. 6:12). Like Moses, Gideon was not so sure this was a mission that he wanted. Like most of us, Gideon considered the world he lived in and wondered, "But sir, if the LORD is with us, why then has all this happened to us?" (v. 13).

Why? Because humanity continues on the path that we chose in the garden. The very structure of the book of Judges is ordered by the cycle of obedience and rejection of God. While Gideon had his doubts and asked God for proofs of his calling, he came to accept that God was indeed with him and would guide him in walking the path before him. He followed God's leading, and "the land had rest forty years in the days of Gideon" (8:28). Gideon himself eventually allowed the power and prestige that he had gained through his initial obedience to lead him into greed and the Israelites into idolatry (Judg. 8:24–27).

Yet God never left the Israelites; indeed, he has never left humanity.

We see this especially when God calls Mary. Like Gideon, when God calls Mary into a time of trial and difficulty, she is told, "The Lord is with you" (Luke 1:28). Everything about Gabriel's announcement to Mary is fraught with fear and anxiety. Betrothed, but not yet married, she is now pregnant. Rather than bringing forty years respite to a portion of Israel, this time the angel declares that the salvation of the world is at hand and will come through Mary. Yet that salvation will only come through the loss of her baby boy. For all the assurance of the angels, I am sure she grieved no less than any other mother. When Gabriel spoke to Mary, he spoke to all the world since, through Mary, Jesus — God's only and eternal son — came into this world, in the language of *The Book of Common Prayer*, "to share our human nature, to live and die as one of us, to reconcile us" to God, the Father of all.[4] His name is Emmanuel, "God with us."

"The LORD be with you" as a greeting is first found in the Bible in the book of Ruth (2:4). It is simple, practically perfunctory, yet full of blessing. "The LORD be with you," Boaz says to his men. In both the Greek of Luke and the Hebrew of Ruth, there is no verb (none is required in those languages) but rather the simple assertion, "The LORD with you." It is awkward in English, yet it conveys more forcefully, to me at least, the fact that it is not a question of past, present, or future; rather, the truth is that wherever and whenever we are, there is the Lord. "The LORD with you." This is the grace of God, the freely given gift that enables us to continue to move through this world, even while looking for the complete healing that will come only in the world to come. Jesus himself offered the same encouragement to the disciples on multiple occasions, most notably in his last words recorded in the Gospel of Matthew: "And remember, I am with you always, to the end of the age" (Matt. 28:20).

Jesus also promised that God would send "the Advocate, the Holy Spirit" to be with us, to teach, comfort, and guide us. The LORD is with us, always. So how do we experience God's presence? How do we hear God speak to us out of the whirlwind, see the face of God, and know that he is with us? The green bean casserole; the cup of coffee brought by our desk just "because"; the text message, card, or note sent to say to a friend, "I am with you." Jesus sent us out into the world to continue his ministry, and the Holy Spirit works through us. Some have and will receive more direct visions and experiences from God, I do not doubt that, but God is no less present with my family and me, who see the face of God in the smile of friends who stop by to share a drink and to share stories about how their son still talks about Mack, still laughs in remembering his antics or the celebration after a great stop he made in the soccer goal (he *was* a great keeper). We abide in the Lord, and he abides in us: God with us.

God is with us, from creation to the new creation. While God was with the man and the woman in the garden, and while God called Moses to bring his people out of Egypt and was present with them on their journey through the wilderness, in Jesus God literally walked with us, through hardships, suffering, and death. We do not, as the author of Hebrews reminds us, have a God who is aloof and apart; rather, Jesus, our high priest, is "one who in every respect has been tested as we are, yet without sin" (Heb. 4:15).

Almighty God, whose most dear Son went not up to joy but first he suffered pain, and entered not into glory before he was crucified: Mercifully grant that we, walking in the way of the cross, may find it none other than the way of life and peace; through Jesus Christ our Lord. Amen.[5]

Reflection Questions

1. Does the analogy of grief as an ill-fitting pair of shoes ring true for you? What are some other metaphors with which you can identify in describing your experience of suffering and grief?
2. How have you found your experience of grief to be unique from the way others mourn the same loss?
3. How have you seen God's provision for your physical needs in difficult times? What are some of the most meaningful offerings or gestures you have received from friends when you are struggling?
4. What biblical examples of "I will be with you" or "God with us" do you find most meaningful? How do you think such promises affected the characters in those stories who faced dangerous or frightening trials?
5. How do you envision or feel God's presence with you in times of trouble? Is it more like the footprints poem's image of God carrying you, like a companion walking alongside you, or like something else entirely?

CHAPTER 6

WALKING IN GRACE

The couple was expecting a child, and all seemed to be going well—until it wasn't. Tragically, their little girl did not survive; the parents grieved her death. Within a few months their pastor took them aside to counsel them. He and others, he assured them, loved them but were concerned for their faith. Three months later they were still grieving the death of their child rather than accepting that it was God's will to take her. If you truly had faith in God's divine providence, he told them, then you would accept even this hardship as a gift from God. Your job is to prayerfully understand why God sent this and what God is teaching you through this time of trial.

You can imagine how devastating this "pastoral counseling" session was to this young couple. They *were* grieving and will continue to do so for their entire lives. Elizabeth, Izzy, and I still grieve the death of Mack, as do so many of our friends and family. Grieving is a natural and necessary part of loss and therefore of life. As I noted at the outset, the idea that Christians should not grieve is misguided on many levels. I have already noted that our confidence in the resurrection does not remove our grief and sadness; rather, it transforms it. We grieve, but not as those without such faith. In this case, the pastor was asserting that their continued grief was evidence that they were lacking in faith, that they did not believe firmly enough that God was in control of every element of their lives and had sent this tragedy for a purpose. This pastor is not a straw man. The experience was shared with me by the couple, and I have since heard from several others who have had similar encounters. It makes sense that we should try to ascribe meaning to our suffering, but for such instances of unmerited trauma, this theological approach has it backward and is harmful. We need to explore not why God has *sent* this to us, but how God is *with* us as we move forward in finding purpose.

This pernicious position is rooted in the view of God's sovereignty, discussed in chapter 2, that asserts that God controls every minute detail of our lives, even sending evil upon us.[1] If we do not accept that the loss of a child or the onset of cancer is from God, the argument goes, then we are lacking in faith. I acknowledge John Piper for walking the path that he teaches in this respect. Just before undergoing surgery for prostate cancer, he wrote, "You will waste your cancer if you do not believe it is designed for you by God."[2] He maintains a firm conviction that *every* bit of suffering is *designed and directed* by God. I obviously disagree and believe that such a belief is based on a misreading of Scripture, but I will grant that if this understanding brings someone comfort and strength in their moment of trial, then I would not challenge it in that moment. I do, however, believe that such teaching can be truly harmful when *imposed* upon others who do not share that particular understanding of God's sovereignty. In fact, I know many people for whom the insistence of such a view within their church community has driven them *away* from the church at precisely the time in their lives when the body of Christ should be most loving and supportive.

When our son died and people told me, "God took Mack for a reason," I understood that they were trying to love me and comfort me. I accepted their words in that spirit, and I am grateful for their love. But had I not had the theological background that I do, I most likely would have been offended and repulsed. I suspect I would have countered, "There can be no justifiable reason to take Mack. Anything God hoped to accomplish by taking my son, an all-powerful God could accomplish in less harmful and destructive means. If *that* is God, then I cannot believe in such a God." There are many people who have made the decision to disbelieve when confronted with such a theological justification of their suffering. Bart Ehrman is perhaps the most famous contemporary example: "I could no longer explain how there can be a good and all-powerful God actively involved with this world, given the state of things. . . . I came to a point where I simply could not believe that there is a good and kindly disposed Ruler who is in charge of it."[3] And I would agree, if that was all there was to it.

The argument that says God takes the life of some innocent person in order to guide or direct another into obedience or better living is incredibly harmful and damaging. Theologian D. A. Carson says, "I know couples who ended up on the mission field because they lost their children, preachers who learned to care when they were first themselves bereaved, senior saints whose Christian influence swelled enormously after they lost all of their children in tragic circumstances. I do not claim to know whether each of these instances should be viewed as examples of God's fatherly discipline. I rather imagine that there was a mixture."[4] An otherwise thoughtful and compassionate scholar and teacher, Carson puts forward this argument that God, sovereign and all-powerful though he may be, somehow has no other options to get these individuals to serve him in the mission field than to take their children. That simply does not fit with any conception of justice that I am aware of; it certainly is not the sort of justice that we find in the Bible. It also does not fit with a view of an omnipotent God; such a God could accomplish those goals in a nondestructive way. God does not discipline the father by making the child suffer.

Tragedy can move and inspire us without being credited to the actions of God. When I was being locally formed to be a priest,[5] I met another, older, newly ordained priest who was a retired Army colonel. He shared the story of how, when stationed at the Pentagon, his commanding officer called him in and gave him the unenviable duty of informing a wife and mother that her husband had been killed on duty. He explained to the general that he was not a counselor or psychologist, that he was not a sympathetic man and was unsuited to the assignment. The general merely tapped his epilates (the indicator of his rank) and said, "This says that it is your assignment." That night my friend's wife died in her sleep. "That night I learned empathy," he said. The experience shaped his life and moved him toward ministry after his career in the military, but he never suggested in any way that God took his wife in order to send him into ministry. Rather, in his grief, he found that God was there with him, comforting him and helping him to understand how his experience could help shape and inform his future life and ministry.

I was fortunate that my prior study and faith experience had already led me to the conclusion that a conception of God's sovereignty such as that put forward by Piper and Carson was not the only possible understanding of Scripture or even an accurate one. Tragedy happens in our lives because of the broken nature of this world, what Carson calls (and gets quite right) the "effluent of the fall."[6] While I grieve the death of my son, I am not at the same time struggling with a crisis of faith. I know that God remains the God of love who is present with us at all times and through all things, even in this world of pain and hurt.

Making Meaning

If God has *not* directly ordained the death of a child or the onset of leukemia, how do we make sense of the hardship and grief we suffer in response to such tragedies? How do we keep moving forward? We did not ask for this to come upon us. We did not ask to become bereaved parents, to battle cancer, or to declare bankruptcy. And yet God is present with us, in our grief and anxiety, in our sorrow and lamentation. In this time of tragedy, we have the opportunity to make our own choices about how we move through that darkened valley and whether or not we acknowledge God's presence and seek out his guidance. God may not have purposefully sent suffering upon us, but God can reveal meaning and purpose for our lives as we grow from that point forward.

Viktor Frankl, a Holocaust survivor and psychologist, wrote in his justly famous work *Man's Search for Meaning* that meaning is found in what we place upon our experience and take from it: "When a man finds that it is his destiny to suffer, he will have to accept his suffering as his task; his single and unique task. He will have to acknowledge the fact that even in suffering he is unique and alone in the universe. No one can relieve him of his suffering or suffer in his place. His unique opportunity lies in the way in which he bears his burden."[7]

The heavy load of grief and sorrow has been placed upon our backs without our will, yet we are not without agency. The choice that remains for us is to decide how we will carry it. We do not choose to have a child die, or to lose a job, or to develop cancer, but we can choose how we respond to those events. In so doing, the suffering itself is transformed; although not forgotten or denuded of its raw power inflicted on our lives, it is altered and changed into an experience, a love, a thing of *our* choosing. It is not, however, something we do alone. We are in community not only with those around us who love us and want to help us carry the load, but with God, our comforter and companion. This is the function of lament—to take to God our burden, express our grief and anger, and seek out his guidance for how best to carry on.

Elizabeth and I arrived in the hospital sometime after midnight. We stayed by Mack's body for several hours, his sister unaware as she enjoyed her sleepover at a friend's house. As we drove back in the darkest part of the night to tell Izzy, we began to talk about how Mack would be remembered, the impact his death would have on Izzy and on his buddies. We have always been in unison that we wanted people to remember *Mack*, and we wanted Izzy to continue to have a healthy, vibrant life. We did not want his death to be remembered as the beginning of the collapse of the Brady family. In fact, it was not his death that we wanted people to remember at all, but his life and his exuberant joy.

So we considered ways to commemorate this bright light. We wanted people, especially his teammates, to celebrate the vibrant, lively boy who was an excellent soccer goalie and a silly, fun friend. By the end of the drive, we had decided to establish a fund for the Penn State Men's Soccer Goalkeepers. Mack had dreamed of playing for Penn State some day and then representing the United States in goal. Because so much of my job involved raising endowments for the university, I knew what it would take (you need at least $50,000 in the account before the interest will pay out for the coach to spend) and that it would likely require several years of our own giving, but we thought it was a fitting tribute to our keeper. What we did not fully comprehend was how important it was for *others* to be able to give, to express their grief and sorrow while also building up something positive and affirming of Mack's spirit. So when the director of development came to the viewing several days later, we were astonished to be told that the fund had already eclipsed the $50,000 mark.

That target had been reached by hundreds and hundreds of small gifts. I am still brought to tears thinking of so many people remembering our boy, many who had never known him. The point in sharing our experience is not to suggest that we are somehow role models of how to handle the loss of a child or to brag about the Mack Fund. I cannot tell you exactly why we thought to take that approach, of seeking a positive and life-affirming memorial of Mack, but we believe that the Spirit led us to seek a way to transform our tragedy into something beautiful. There is a reason the butterfly is used as a symbol by so many bereaved parents.

Somehow we have to find a way to move forward *with* our tragedy (not *from*, as we can never leave it behind). Since we cannot change the reality of our loss, it is vital that we attempt to bring some meaning to our journey. If we must walk through the dark valley of the shadow of death, we must make sure we do not dwell too long in it, or we might become overwhelmed and lose our way. Tabitha Kapic was diagnosed with and then overcame cancer and now lives with erythromelalgia, an incredibly painful disease that leaves her in near constant pain. Her husband, Kelly Kapic, is a theologian who has written *Embodied Hope*, a powerful and moving theological reflection on pain and suffering.[8] In an interview on the podcast *The Table*, Kapic shared that Tabitha compares suffering to geography, to a place rather than a time. I find this to be powerfully true. While I know the day and time in the past when Mack died, it is also a place that I can go and visit in my mind and spirit. It is a place of deepest darkness and a place wherein it is far too easy to get lost. Such places are OK to visit occasionally, but we must be careful not to remain there too long, and as we travel the dark terrain, we need to reach out for the staff of God to guide and comfort us. We may do this in honest prayer, lament, and simple tears, but in opening our hearts to the memories and the spirit of our loved ones, we must be open to God's leading us forward as well.

Forward in Purpose

There's an important distinction to be made between *meaning* and *purpose*, which are highly interrelated but are not quite the same thing. In general, seeking meaning in or from an experience requires reflecting back upon the event. Purpose in life, on the other hand, looks forward, builds upon the meaning derived from experience, and helps motivate and drive us into the future. It involves more than just understanding something; it requires doing. When we affirm that God is present with us as we continue in this world, we must do so with meaning and purpose; in so doing, we will find our tragedy being transformed into hope. It is a shift from the passive and reactive to the active and directive.

The book of Ruth offers an excellent example of one who was in grief and yet found purpose in living forward, into the future. The story is set in the time of the judges, and it opens with Bethlehem, "the house of bread," in famine while Elimelech and his wife, Naomi, are "full" with a family of two sons, Mahlon and Chilion. To avoid the famine, Elimelech moves his family to Moab, a historical enemy of Israel, and they remain there for a number of years. Naomi's life changes tragically when her husband dies and she is left with her two sons. The sons marry Moabite women, Orpah and Ruth, but then they too die, leaving Naomi, Orpah, and Ruth widows. With no future in Moab and the famine having ended in Judah, Naomi resolves to return home to Bethlehem. Her daughter-in-law Orpah turns back, but Ruth resolves to stay with Naomi and go with her to Israel.

Naomi is a widow and a bereaved parent. She has lost her husband and her sons and must now fend for herself. Ruth is a young widow and a foreigner, a stranger from an enemy land. They are among the most vulnerable in society—which is why the law repeatedly calls upon Israel to "care for the widow, the orphan, and the stranger in your midst"—and their prospects are poor. When they arrive in Bethlehem, the women of the town barely recognize Naomi, she has so changed. Naomi cannot bear it: "Call me no longer Naomi, call me Mara, for the Almighty has dealt bitterly with me. I went away full, but the LORD has brought me back empty; why call me Naomi when the LORD has dealt harshly with me, and the Almighty has brought calamity upon me?" (Ruth 1:20–21). So ends chapter 1. Chapter 2 opens with Naomi understandably depressed and despondent.

We can envision the scene as Naomi sits in the corner of the small, dark place she and Ruth have been offered as shelter. What else is there for her to do? All is gone, and it is the Lord who has done this to her. Ruth is having none of it: "Let me go to the field and glean among the ears of grain, behind someone in whose sight I may find favor" (Ruth 2:2). Ruth does not stay in that dark place for long. She makes a plan; she takes action.

Ruth is also in the midst of the gloom of grief. Her husband died as well as Naomi's, and now she is a foreigner living in a land of strangers, a point driven home by the fact that everyone refers to her as "that Moabite girl" (v. 6), yet Ruth steps up and out to provide for herself and Naomi. She takes action, she chooses not to remain in the midst of their personal devastation but to move forward. Notice how Ruth is deliberative and constructive in her action. She considers their need and her capacity, what she is capable of doing as a foreign woman living in this land. The law said that landowners had to leave the corners of the field or the fallen grapes in the vineyard "for the poor and the alien" to glean. This was something constructive and productive that Ruth could do that would not only get her out of the house and keep her active, but would provide for their immediate, practical needs.

I am certainly no psychologist, but I have been through enough grief and depression, as well as being alongside others who have walked in the valley, that I know the importance of not getting stuck in a moment. Today we are fortunate to know that some forms of depression and anxiety are biologically and chemically based and can be treated as such. Often, as is the case with Ruth and Naomi and me, the creeping sadness of depression comes from circumstances in life, such as losing a husband or a child, a job or a home.

In those circumstances we are right to take stock with Naomi, to see the reality of the world we inhabit, which is full of both blessings and burdens. But we can't stay there too long; it is a dark, dank room that will sap us of all vitality. One of the best things we can do is get up—to really, physically, get up and get moving. We need to move physically in space and mentally in our thoughts and visions. To be physically active changes the chemical makeup of our brains; it starts what the *Harvard Health Letter* calls "a biological cascade of events" that begins to lift us up in body and mind.[9] It changes our vantage point and helps us to gain a broader perspective, to see God in creation and to hear his voice through those around us and the opportunities presented to us.

Ruth, seeing the situation and having spent her time in mourning, is ready to go out into the light of day and work in the fields to ensure that she and her mother-in-law have the food that they need. And, she tells Naomi, perhaps she will find "someone in whose sight I may find favor." Boaz has been introduced in the first verse of chapter 2, so we know that he will find Ruth in his field and that he will, indeed, favor her. We should not lose sight, however, that it is Ruth who drives the narrative, both of the story and her life, and takes the initiative to step out and receive the future and the life that is proffered for herself and Naomi.

God is present, even and especially in the dark room of depression. But God also calls us out to meet Christ in others and in the circumstances of life. It is perhaps the hardest step and one that we do not take alone; God goes ahead of us, walks alongside us, and dwells within us.

When Mack died, my wife and I were very intentional about giving our daughter space and support in her grief, providing outlets for our own grief (including nightly two-mile walks together, which were often full of tears and few words), and ensuring that Mack was remembered for himself, his joys, and his enthusiasm, not for his death and its impact on our lives. We chose to walk from that place of darkness and sorrow with purpose, to celebrate his life and to continue to live life fully. And we did so confident not only that God was with us, but that Mack was with God. Again, I do not mean to set us up as an example of strength or to suggest that it was not the most difficult thing we have ever done. It was. It has been as hard as any challenge one can face, and we have not been perfect or always at peace in the struggle. But I do believe firmly that our spiritual, emotional, and relational health begins with making such intentional and purposeful decisions.

Heavenly Father, in you we live and move and have our being: We humbly pray that you guide and govern us by your Holy Spirit, that in all the cares and occupations of our life we may not forget you, but may remember that we are ever walking in your sight; through Jesus Christ our Lord. Amen.[10]

Reflection Questions

1. In what ways have you tried to make sense of suffering and loss for yourself or others? Have others found these understandings helpful or not?
2. How have you or others in your life been changed by suffering and loss? Do you see the hand of God in that change? How so?

3. What actions have you taken to make something meaningful come out of senseless tragedy?
4. Have there been moments in your grief journey when you felt stuck like Naomi? Do you still feel that way? How did you (or could you) start moving again, taking action?
5. What does moving forward with purpose look like for you?

CHAPTER 7

LIVING IN THE
MOMENT

In 2000, U2 came out with their tenth studio album, *All That You Can't Leave Behind*. The album will always be poignant to me because I was playing it in my car on September 11, 2001. We were living in Covington, Louisiana, and I had been taking my time getting ready in the morning since I had jury duty and would not need to go across Lake Pontchartrain to my office at Tulane University that day. Then NPR interrupted its programming to announce what they thought, what everyone hoped, was a tragic accident. We turned on the television and watched it unfold, and as the full scope of the attacks became clear, I received a notice that all courthouses and state buildings were closed. There would be no jury duty that day. I decided to head into the office after all. I wanted to be present in case any of my students, many of whom were from the New York City area and had parents and family who worked in the city, needed to talk. As I drove across the twenty-four-mile-long Lake Pontchartrain Causeway, the sky was crystal clear. There was no air traffic coming in or out of the New Orleans

airport, or any in the country. I put the new U2 album into my little Honda Civic's cassette player, and Bono's soaring words of the first track, "Beautiful Day," echoed the beauty I saw around me and clashed with the reality unfolding in our country.

> It's a beautiful day
> Don't let it get away

Maybe it is because I am a product of my time and generation, but I really love U2. This album represents so much of what I love about their lyrics and lyricism, and I consider it one of their best, or at least one of my favorites. It is another song on that album, however, that continues to speak deeply to me. Passionate and musically evocative, "Stuck in a Moment You Can't Get Out Of" takes on a deeper meaning when we learn that Bono wrote it as an argument he wished he had had with his friend Michael Hutchence before he committed suicide. It is tender and yet firm:

> Oh love, look at you now.
> You've got yourself stuck in a moment
> and you can't get out of it.

Whether it is grief, depression, sadness, or anxiety, at one time or another we can all find ourselves stuck in a moment and feel like we can't get out. My college years were perhaps the most stressful for me in this respect. I was struggling with the reality that my dreams of being a "real doctor" were not going to become a reality; I went into depression and found myself feeling like my head was going to explode. (I have no idea what that really means, but that was often how I would describe it.) Years later, while listening to this song, I believed that Bono was expressing exactly my feelings; I was stuck in a moment that I felt I couldn't get out of. The ability to survive such

times is to step outside of that moment, to find a way to gain a broader perspective and see the full view of our life. It is imperative we recognize that these moments are just that—moments that will pass—and that we can survive and move beyond this moment.

Since high school, I have been fortunate in having a mentor, Arnie, who is also a psychiatrist. A friend of my parents, he is just between us in terms of age. In my high school years, I would babysit his children, do yard work for him, and then sit and talk with him about dreams and goals. I went to Cornell University in no small part because he had gone to Cornell and Cornell Med. As I encountered those emotional challenges in my freshman year, he advised that I should go to the university health center and talk with a mental health counselor. It was an important and significant moment in my life for many reasons, foremost because my friend, a devout Christian himself, encouraged me to get the psychological support I needed and affirmed that such counseling does not in any way run counter to the Christian faith. The importance of mental health care has stayed with me, and I am a strong advocate for it within universities, in particular, to ensure that our students, faculty, and staff have access to the resources they need to live a fully healthy life, mentally and physically.

That meeting in my freshman year was notable for another reason. When I sat down next to the counselor's desk, he asked the question that I now know counselors are required to ask of all students they meet with: Have you thought about taking your own life? I replied, honestly, yes. He asked if I had ever made any efforts or attempts at suicide, and I said no, I had not. Why? I can remember my response quite vividly because even at the time I thought it sounded awfully simplistic and naive: "I am a Christian, and I believe that God created me for a purpose. It is not up to me to short-change that. I have to see this through." I believed it then, and I believe it now. My theology is much more nuanced now, and I can add many layers to the reasons for sticking around, but I still firmly believe that my job is to be *here* right now. The counselor didn't seem to have quite the same view of the world.

He replied, "I don't get it. Why haven't you tried to take your own life?"

I thanked him and then left the center. I did *not* walk away from counseling. It is important to say again that mental health counseling, whether by psychologists, psychiatrists, or counselors, is—for many people—not just the right thing to do but is something vital to their well-being and does not, in any way, run counter to the Christian faith. That is why, after leaving the university health center and chatting with Arnie, he helped me find a Christian psychiatrist. It may not be necessary for everyone, but for me it was important to have a counselor who shared my worldview. We need such friends and counselors because they help us step outside of that moment; they can lift the needle off the scratched record that just keeps repeating and repeating and repeating. As Christians we grieve, but not in the same way as those who have no faith in the resurrection. So too, we will struggle with sadness, depression, and perhaps even other mental health issues, yet we do so in the awareness of God's larger plan for our lives. We know that this world is not all there is, that we are made for eternity; yet we also know that we have a place and a role here, now, in the present.

While I have argued above that God does not dictate every single moment of our lives, there is no doubt that Scripture affirms that God knows and cares about us and our choices and seeks to use us as his presence of grace in this world. God reveals himself to us through creation and those around us, so God uses us to be his presence in the lives of others. By God's grace and often with the help of others, we can and will step out of that moment, walk through that dark passage. This time will pass.

"Change the channel" was Arnie's analogy. It is not just okay to experience those moments of grief and sadness; it is healthy, but you need to change the channel before too long. Always one with practical advice, Arnie said it is just like television: we need to change our view, and sometimes the very best way to do that is to physically get up and move. When you find yourself overwhelmed with grief, allow the emotion to run through you, but then get up, leave that room, go outside for a walk, make a cup of tea, change the channel.

Many were the times as I wrote this book when I was overwhelmed with the memory of Mack or with thoughts about the sorrow of our friends whose daughter died in the riding accident. I thought of my father, who lived a good, full life, but also my mother, who grieves his absence deeply. When such a moment happens, I take the moment, feel it, and often curse the fact that this is where I find myself, and then I get up from the desk and do *something* — anything — to change the channel.

Often I simply take the dog for a walk. (She is a very fit dog.)

Study after study has shown that one of the most effective treatments for depression and grief is physical activity. Shortly after Mack died, we got Lady Molly O'Brady, an apricot toy poodle that is one of the silliest dogs you will meet (she spins in circles when she is excited). It was something we had been contemplating for years, but having Lady had the unexpected benefit of getting us out of ourselves and our house. (This was not an unexpected benefit to Arnie, who encouraged us to go ahead with our plans.) Elizabeth and I continued to take our nightly two-mile walks, but now with a ball of fluff along as well. Change the channel, get out of your normal space, take time to be with others who know your grief and are willing to let you talk about it or not.

While it is imperative that we do not allow ourselves to *remain in* any one moment, there is value in *living in* the moment. It is healthy and appropriate to feel fully the weight of guilt and sorrow, joy and exultation. After

Mack died, Arnie was one of the first people to call us and visit with us. He wisely counseled us, saying that we should not try and avoid our feelings or control our feelings. They are what they are, and they will come, falling upon us unbidden and sometimes violently like a summer thunderstorm. Allow yourself to be in *that moment*, he said. It is good for us to experience the fullness of our humanity, including all the feelings. Jesus did as well, not only weeping and grieving over the death of his friend and the rebellion of God's people, but also suffering under the weight of hardships and just being human. He was "in every respect has been tested as we are, yet without sin" (Heb. 4:15). We should take strength from that, knowing that Jesus knows and shares our suffering and will help us through those times.

A Time to Heal, a Time to Laugh

It can feel wrong to continue to enjoy life when your child is no longer with you. We miss and grieve our loved ones not simply because they are not with us, but because we had plans and visions for a future with them. At first, after Mack died, everything seemed wrong without him, because it was. We had talked of getting a dog. When we got Lady, Mack was not there to help us pick her out. (Or to object, since she was this little fluffball, and his buddy had a big German shepherd! We are certain Mack would have loved Lady but equally certain he would have thought she was too silly and cuddly.) Every time we took a trip together or had a family gathering, every time we made memories without Mack, it was jarring, felt wrong, and brought tears. He should have been with us. To be doing something, anything, without our loved one can feel wrong. Yet we cannot allow ourselves to feel guilty about continuing to live, continuing to enjoy the life that we have — not least because they remain a part of our lives. You will *never* forget a loved one. Going on a holiday is not a sign that you are no longer grieving, because you will think about that person with every selfie you take.

As we continue to live, we continue to celebrate our loved one. For example, it is proper and prayerful to commemorate their birthday and the anniversary of their death. We have no English term for the latter, but I often borrow the Yiddish term *Jahrzeit*. It simply means "anniversary" but is now used exclusively to refer to the anniversary of the death of a close member of the family (parent, sibling, or spouse) for whom the mourner would say the Kaddish, the prayer for the deceased on the anniversary of their death.[1] Consider finding the right way for you and your family to celebrate such occasions. For example, my brother-in-law and his wife give each of their children a LEGO set on Mack's birthday (and they send us a picture). I regularly light a candle as I give thanks to God and remember Mack and my father and the brightness of their light in our lives.

You will find all sorts of ways, big and small, to both grieve and heal, to remember and move forward. One of the most painful moments I had in the months after Mack's death was the first time I took a business trip. I had always picked up a trinket for our children when I traveled. Our daughter would get a small snow globe and Mack would get a keychain. He would put them on a carabiner on his backpack (a backpack that often had nothing else in it, humorously weighed down by nearly two dozen key chains). After his death, his friend that he sat with on the bus told us that every time Mack got a new key chain, he would tell her all about it and where I had been. (She was also his "girlfriend" in the way that eight-year-olds are. In her grief, she asked her mom, "Do you think my husband will be jealous of Mack?") In O'Hare airport while waiting for my flight, I went into the gift shop to get the snow globe and key chain. I didn't even think about it. For a split second Mack was still alive, still waiting at home for me to come back with a new key chain and a new story of where I had been. Holding the key chain in my hand, reality smashed into my chest and took my breath away. I practically ran out of the store and called Elizabeth sobbing. She said, "Buy the key chain. Remember Mack and buy the key chain." I did. I do. Sitting on my desk right now is a carabiner with twenty-one key chains on it and another carabiner already full from the three years after his death. We continue the tradition and remember Mack with each new addition. Several are key chains that Izzy, who has studied abroad twice in the last two years, has brought back for Mack and for me to add to the collection. In so doing, we are saying a prayer of thanksgiving for Mack. Like a rosary, each key chain is a prayer, a memory of a place Izzy or I have been and a time, in that place, when we remembered Mack. He is with us.

Living in each moment means an awareness that this life is the "merest breath," as Qohelet says in Ecclesiastes. It is fleeting and, unless we infuse it with meaning, can seem pointless; nihilism can become overwhelming. Qohelet also counsels that this is why we should enjoy and cherish the moments that we have. This is all the more true when grief has entered our lives. Each moment is a new opportunity to receive God's love and grace as we seek out the purpose and meaning for our lives and the lives that we carry with us.

Morning by Morning

Most Christians' main exposure to the book of Lamentations is through the hymn "Great Is Thy Faithfulness," which is based upon Lamentations 3:22–24. It is sung in all sorts of services, from weddings to funerals, because it contains basic truths about God's never-ending and never-failing love for us. The biblical foundation of the hymn is from the very center of the book of Lamentations, a position that is no accident. While the book itself brings the complaint to God for the destruction of Jerusalem (chapter 3 opens with the wrenching line "I am one who has seen affliction under the rod of God's wrath"), at its heart is the confession of faith that God will not punish the people forever, but will have mercy: "The steadfast love of the LORD never ceases, his mercies never come to an end; they are new every morning; great is your faithfulness" (Lam. 3:22–23).Every morning, every moment, God's mercy and love are poured out for us. Living in the moment, rather than being stuck in a moment, is living in the center of God's love and mercy.

That is where those of us who grieve or suffer often find ourselves, taking it one step at a time, one day at a time. The sun rising on a new day can often bring with it the simple, painful awareness that our loved one is still not with us, that our illness is still with us. The passage of time doesn't lessen our grief; it just changes it. I still frequently wake up feeling like a brick is on my chest as I realize that Mack is gone. That is often my very first thought of the day. "His mercies are new every morning" is a refrain I need to hear, I need to repeat, I need to claim.

Perhaps that is why I so often select this particular collect from Morning Prayer:

O God, the King eternal, whose light divides the day from the night and turns the shadow of death into the morning: Drive far from us all wrong desires, incline our hearts to keep your law, and guide our feet into the way of peace; that, having done your will with cheerfulness while it was day, we may, when night comes, rejoice to give you thanks; through Jesus Christ our Lord. Amen.[2]

Most of this is, let's be honest, a good but mundane prayer that we will serve God during the day. The opening clause, however, speaks to me profoundly as I pray to the God "whose light divides the day from the night and turns the shadow of death into the morning." I need that reassurance and I need to confess, to confirm each morning that God *is* the one who continues to bless, continues to have mercy, and is faithful even, and especially, when I am not. It also reflects that tension we live in as Christians, acknowledging the importance of living today, in this world, while affirming that this world is not all that there is and that there will *always* be a tomorrow, a world to come.

This emphasis on living in and through this present moment appears several times in the New Testament. In Hebrews, the author quotes Psalm 95:7 to inspire his audience to comfort each other in their struggles: "But exhort one another every day, as long as it is called 'today,' so that none of you may be hardened by the deceitfulness of sin. . . . As it is said, 'Today, if you hear his voice, do not harden your hearts as in the rebellion'" (Heb. 3:13, 15). It is not just that the author wants his audience to be obedient; rather, he wants us to receive fully the grace and peace offered to us, to "enter into the rest" in Christ. We have limited time here in this world, so do not delay! While it is "today," take hold of the promises of God and find true sabbath rest.

The "deceitfulness of sin" that he warns of is the lie that this world is all there is and that we will not and cannot have rest and peace. It is the lie that all the world has to offer is heartache and suffering. This is, in fact, the section that culminates in the reminder and promise that because Jesus is our great high priest who has experienced all the suffering and hardship of this life as we have, today we can "approach the throne of grace with boldness, so that we may receive mercy and find grace to help in time of need" (Heb. 4:16).

Paul also emphasizes this same sense of the "nowness" and the constant repetition of God's grace as he urges his audience to persevere in the now: "For [the LORD] says, 'At an acceptable time I have listened to you, and on a day of salvation I have helped you' [Isa. 49:8]. See, now is the acceptable time; see, now is the day of salvation!" (2 Cor. 6:2). Preachers often focus upon the imperative tone of Paul's words in order to call us to conversion, but Paul is writing to the church at Corinth, not preaching in the Areopagus. This audience has already accepted Jesus as Christ. Paul is not seeking to convert them but to encourage them to stand firm and endure the hardships that inevitably come in life. Christ reconciles us to God and in so doing calls us to be his "ambassadors." The time of our work in Christ is *now*; not some far off future day of the Lord, but this moment. Every moment is now.

The argument of the letter is to call the Corinthian Christians into faithful action *and* to encourage them in their own time of suffering. Paul opens with an invocation and a confirmation of our struggles and our hope: "Blessed be the God and Father of our Lord Jesus Christ, the Father of mercies and the God of all consolation. . . . For just as the sufferings of Christ are abundant for us, so also our consolation is abundant through Christ" (2 Cor. 1:3, 5). In fact, our encouragement and consolation come through our service to God and others. Paul says that God "consoles us in all our affliction, so that we may be able to console those who are in any affliction with the consolation with which we ourselves are consoled by God" (2 Cor. 1:4). It may be that we are more empathetic to those who suffer illness, divorce, or grief after we have gone through it ourselves. Yet if we accept the grace and peace of Christ, then we will enjoy and be able to share something much greater than empathy: consolation. This is the same term (*parakaleo*) we find in Hebrews translated as "encouragement" or "exhortation." That encouragement or consolation comes from the fact that Jesus has transformed death from an end into a beginning. Through Jesus, our suffering and grief in this world will become joy and life in the World to Come.

This knowledge does not remove the pain and sorrow of our struggles in this moment, but it provides us with a more complete perspective on our life, like being in a high tower and seeing the whole valley laid out before us. What has been revealed to us, and what Qohelet did not know, is that this world is not the end, that it is not all there is to life. I would even suggest that referring to what occurs after we die as the "afterlife" is misleading, since that is when the fullness of our life actually begins! When we find ourselves in difficult and challenging moments, overwhelmed with grief or anxiety, we should lift our eyes up to see the broad expanse of life that is before us in Christ, as Paul encourages the Corinthians:

> So we do not lose heart. Even though our outer nature is wasting away, our inner nature is being renewed day by day. For this slight momentary affliction is preparing us for an eternal weight of glory beyond all measure, because we look not at what can be seen but at what cannot be seen; for what can be seen is temporary, but what cannot be seen is eternal. (2 Cor. 4:16–18)

It is our calling as ambassadors of Christ to call others to this truth: that we have eternity before us. These moments we live in now are vital, and God is present with us, granting us grace and peace as we walk through them. When the terrain becomes rocky and the way is hard, God consoles us and offers us encouragement in the knowledge that this is temporary and just the beginning.

;

This does not, however, mean that we should rush through this time to get to the next! Our time here now is valuable, and we must live fully in it. One of the tragic aspects of college life is that each year there are students who are in anguish and who struggle to see the purpose of their remaining in this world any longer. They find themselves trapped in that moment, and they believe there is only one way out of it. Sadly, I have been to several funerals for young people who felt they had no other options. At such times, one of the most important messages we can convey to their friends and peers is that we need them, the survivors, *here*. They are still needed here, as challenging and difficult as it is; they are needed and loved. A visual reminder of just this point is the semicolon, a punctuation mark signifying a pause between statements that are distinct but still one sentence. Survivors of depression or loss often have a semicolon tattooed somewhere where they can see it regularly to remind them that this particular moment, no matter how dark or dire, is not a period, is not the end; rather, it is just a pause. I think that captures it beautifully.

Paul writes about our future hope of the resurrection more than any other biblical author, and while he intends it for encouragement, for some people, their faith in the resurrection can lead them to feel they are just marking time here in this world. My father took our son's death very hard. He entered into depression and never emerged. He is one who would never have considered suicide, yet he also never considered counseling. Dad took great comfort in the knowledge that Mack is more than well—that his perishable, physical body had been replaced by his imperishable, spiritual body—and that they would be reunited. Still, he struggled to live fully in his final years not simply because of age and illness, but because he remained stuck in a moment. Perhaps it was because he knew he was so close to his own "homegoing," as some like to call it. Had this tragedy occurred to Dad earlier in his life, I think he would have had the fortitude to meet it and continue to live more fully. But for some, at any age, the burden of missing their loved one, which all who are bereaved bear, can become overwhelming. Into those moments we need to shine the light of the resurrection as a present joy and future hope. The knowledge of the resurrection should be consolation and encouragement, a source of confidence and an impetus to love and share that truth with others.

The gospel of Christ opens to us a new reality, a new awareness of time: God loves us and is present with us now, in this moment, and for all eternity. Every moment is unique and our own, and we need to live into it fully, but always with the awareness that it is all part of our larger life in Christ that extends beyond this world into the next. Those of us who are bereaved now live not only to remember our loved ones who have died, but to proclaim the death and resurrection of the one who has conquered death. We walk forward from that moment of tragedy confident that God is our guide and shepherd and will lead us to our purpose if we are willing to listen for his voice. In the meantime, we share the purpose of all Christians to be ambassadors of Christ, declaring the resurrection and the life of the World to Come.

O God, the protector of all who trust in you, without whom nothing is strong, nothing is holy: Increase and multiply upon us your mercy; that, with you as our ruler and guide, we may so pass through things temporal, that we lose not the things eternal; through Jesus Christ our Lord, who lives and reigns with you and the Holy Spirit, one God, for ever and ever. Amen.[3]

Reflection Questions

1. What are some practical suggestions you have for "changing the channel" when you feel stuck? How do you remind yourself to live fully, even in grief?
2. Do you ever feel guilty for enjoying life or carrying on with plans after the loss of your loved one? In what ways do you commemorate that person's life and memory?
3. Find the words to "Great Is Thy Faithfulness" online or in a hymnal. How do these words speak to you? What other songs, Scripture passages, or prayers do you find encouraging?

4. Consider this verse: "For just as the sufferings of Christ are abundant for us, so also our consolation is abundant through Christ" (2 Cor. 1:5). What does it mean that "the sufferings of Christ are abundant for us"? How do those sufferings become our consolation?

5. Does the semicolon and its meaning of pausing or transitioning—as opposed to ending—resonate with you? If you told your life story in a sentence, what words would come before the semicolon and what words would come after?

CHAPTER 8

RAISED IMPERISHABLE

When I teach courses on the Bible, one of the first interpretive rules I put forward is this: the Bible doesn't answer
all the questions that we want to ask. My go-to example is
"Whom did Cain marry?" Cain, Adam and Eve's eldest son,
killed his brother Abel. As a result, God exiled him, saying,
"You will be a fugitive and a wanderer on the earth" (Gen.
4:12). Just five verses later, with no other explanation, we
read, "Cain knew his wife, and she conceived and bore
Enoch." So far as we know from the biblical account up to
this point, there are only three people on the earth: Adam,
Eve, and Cain. Whom did Cain marry? The Bible doesn't
tell us. We might speculate, coming up with all sorts of
explanations and rationalizations, and frankly that can be
kind of fun.[1] But we only have what the biblical text tells
us, and it is not concerned with that particular question.

There are so many different questions that we would
like answers to that the Bible does not address fully or to
our modern satisfaction. One of the questions that most of
us have at some point is, "What happens when we die?"
I don't mean our ultimate status, as we are assured of the

resurrection throughout the New Testament, but the Bible doesn't give us any sort of detailed answer to the question of what happens to us at the moment when our physical body ceases to function. Popular imagery suggests our soul flies immediately heavenward, appearing promptly at the pearly gates for admission. But this is not an image confirmed in Scripture. As Qohelet says, "Who knows whether the human spirit goes upward and the spirit of animals goes downward to the earth?" (Eccl. 3:21).

In the Old Testament, there is generally the assumption that the spirit of everyone goes "down to Sheol" more or less immediately, but that too is not clearly stated. Sheol is not hell or a place for the condemned, but a "gray place" where all go and are at rest. The only glimpse we receive of Sheol is when Saul has the medium of Endor "bring up" Samuel from the dead (1 Sam. 28). Samuel comes up out of the ground and appears much the same as he did before he died. The woman describes what she sees: "An old man is coming up; he is wrapped in a robe" (v. 14). Samuel asks, "Why have you disturbed me by bringing me up?" (v. 15). There is little more to be gleaned from this episode. The great prophet Samuel has died and is at rest in Sheol. Job, Psalms, and Proverbs refer to Sheol in very general terms as well, in many cases simply as a poetic reference to the moment of death itself.

The resurrection of the dead and the day of judgment are Jewish concepts, however, and are found in the book of Daniel: "Many of those who sleep in the dust of the earth shall awake, some to everlasting life, and some to shame and everlasting contempt. Those who are wise shall shine like the brightness of the sky, and those who lead many to righteousness, like the stars forever and ever" (Dan. 12:2–3). Whether or not there was a bodily resurrection was a major debate within first-century Judaism, as seen in the conflict between the Sadducees and the Pharisees in the Gospels. (To quote my father, "The Sadducees did *not* believe in the resurrection of the dead. Therefore, they were sad, you see?") Jesus and Paul shared the view of the Pharisees, that all would be raised from the dead for the day of judgment, when all would be held to account for their actions.

Paul refers to those who have died as having "fallen asleep." In so doing, he is making the point that our death, as real and final as it is in this world, is just a temporary state before we awaken to new and eternal life in Christ. The New Revised Standard Version masks this by rendering the term as "died," but Paul uses this expression often and with purpose. For example, in talking about the resurrection in 1 Corinthians 15, he says, "Christ has been raised from the dead, the first fruits of those who have died" (v. 20). There are actually two different Greek words for the single English word used in the NRSV (always a poor decision in translation). In the first case, it is the word for "dead," *nekron*. The emphasis is upon the fact that Jesus was *really* dead and yet was raised to life again. "Those who have died" are described as "those who have fallen asleep" (*kekoime menon*). So the sentence is better rendered as "Christ has been raised from the dead, the first fruits of those who have fallen asleep." Paul is emphasizing the fact that Jesus *died*, the death we all must follow, but that as he rose from the dead he transformed our death into a mortal sleep that will be followed by life eternal.

Yet we still have no clear explanation of what happens to us when we die.

I suggest that this is not an accident. We know that humans have always been interested in what happens when we die. The fact that we do not find this topic explored — or to use a better word, *revealed* — in Scripture strongly suggests to me that it is a subject we should best leave alone. I don't mean that we should not think about what has happened to our loved one or what will happen to us; I think about that all the time. What I mean is that the truth about the *moment* of death, that transition, is unknowable — or, at least, it is not revealed in the Bible. Jesus, the only one who could tell us about it, chose not to. What Jesus *did* tell us is that "in my father's house there are many dwelling places" and "I go to prepare a place for you" (John 14:2). (My Uncle Freddie never liked the newer translations, preferring the grandeur of the KJV. He said, "I have been promised a mansion, and I want my mansion!" I feel confident he is not dissatisfied.) The mechanics of death and resurrection are absent—surprisingly so, since they are a central tenet of our faith—and that tells me that our focus ought to be on living *this* life in the *promise* of the resurrection.

The Day of the Lord

Even if the Bible does not provide details about the mechanisms of the resurrection, it contains considerable material that speaks about the fact that *all* will be raised from the dead. When that occurs, the kingdom of God will be established and we will, having had our say and choice in this world, live as God intended us when the cosmos was created. Today's preaching and teaching, however, is often missing a key element of the doctrine of the resurrection: God's judgment.

From the prophets Isaiah and Jeremiah to Daniel, from Jesus to the book of Revelation, the resurrection of the dead is inextricably linked within Scripture to God's final judgment. It is called the "day of the LORD" in the prophets because it is the day on which the LORD God will deliver the faithful and bring judgment upon the wicked. Daniel describes it this way in his concluding vision: "There shall be a time of anguish, such as has never occurred since nations first came into existence. But at that time your people shall be delivered, everyone who is found written in the book. Many of those who sleep in the dust of the earth shall awake, some to everlasting life, and some to shame and everlasting contempt" (Dan. 12:1–2). The concept of God judging, and the consequential condemnation, makes people very uncomfortable today, and I think that is a good thing. Calls for the death penalty and harsh vengeance are *not* signs of God's grace and mercy, so it is a positive movement to see humanity beginning to question our competence at meting out justice, well, justly, and to embrace the value of forgiveness. There are many issues, critical and theological, with regard to these apocalyptic texts that are beyond the scope of this study. It suffices to say for now that I rest in the firm belief that God *is* just and that Jesus "will come again in glory to judge the living and the dead, and his kingdom will have no end," as the Nicene Creed states it. As discomforting as it is to think of the day of judgment, we cannot ignore the fact that Jesus spoke more of this time of judgment than any other figure in the New Testament. His parables about the kingdom of God often included not just the wedding feast, but the casting out of those who had not accepted the invitation of the king. Why is this important, and why is it relevant for the resurrection? Because it is about the injustice that we all see and recognize in this world finally being set right. On that day, we will be raised from the dead so that God can set in order that which is in disorder, mourning will turn into joy, and anguish will be transformed into elation, bitterness into gratitude, and anger into love.

I began this book with the story of Mack's death, something that was tragic, unmerited, and completely normal for this world. And that normalcy is offensive. Others have experienced far greater injustice. Just today, as I write this, a young man decided to indiscriminately shoot people who were at a food festival. Three people were killed; the youngest was six years old. I know of students who have been sexually violated so badly that they can no longer function in society without great anxiety and distress. All grief that we experience, whether from death, violence, ruptured relationships, or physical illness, ultimately comes from the fact that we live in *this* world. It is what it is. But when we are raised from the dead, it will not be to have a party and to celebrate, but for God to establish the new creation; the world itself will be transformed. The Day of the Lord is when all of these injustices will be wiped away. It is not about the wicked *people*; it is the day when evil itself will cease to exist. This world will be transformed into the new heaven and new earth, and *then* we will celebrate! Then we will truly live as we were meant to live. That is just the beginning.

Put on Immortality

In the months following Mack's death, I would not say that I had a crisis of faith, but I certainly felt a general malaise. I was writing about Mack's death and my faith in his/our resurrection, and at the same time there was no doubt that I felt a pall over me. Then we decided to go to my parents' church for Easter. The reading for the sermon was from 1 Corinthians 15, a passage I knew well, but when the pastor read it and began preaching, it was as if I was hearing it for the first time: "For if the dead are not raised, then Christ has not been raised. If Christ has not been raised, your faith is futile and you are still in your sins. Then those also who have died [*Greek:* are asleep] in Christ have perished. If for this life only we have hoped in Christ, we are of all people most to be pitied" (1 Cor. 15:16–19). This is the heart of our faith: Christ has died, Christ has risen, Christ will come again. Did I believe it or not?

Everything hangs upon the resurrection of Christ. With his resurrection, *everything* changed. We still live in a broken world with all the consequences of the fall, but we can now answer Qohelet's question (Eccl. 3:21) and affirm that the human spirit *will* be raised. In that moment in the pew of the church I grew up in, it was all new again. I had to ask myself, Why have I believed in the resurrection of Jesus? Why do I preach and teach it? If I only believed in it for the impact it made on this life, if it was just to inspire myself and others to love one another and to be gracious even to the most ungracious of people, then I would be among those people who are most to be pitied. Believing in the resurrection should mean believing that this world is not all that there is. Yes, the risen Christ in our lives means that we are to love the most unlovely, but it also means that there is something more to live for than just this world. Yes, I realized all over again, I do believe. I wept because Mack was still gone, ripped from us in such a cruel if quiet way, but I wept because it also means that I know I shall go to him.

This was not a crisis of faith, but rather the life of faith, the ebb and flow that can come at any point in one's life. The death of a loved one, especially such an untimely death, naturally brings us back to these moments of asking ourselves, "Do I really believe?" When you find yourself in this situation, and in all likelihood you will at some point, remember that to question God, to be angry, to be disappointed, to feel abandoned is not showing a lack of or a weak faith. It is the sign of resilience and resistance.

We are resilient in that we are questioning, recognizing that not everything is clear-cut and that we are willing to dive into the murky, real world of our emotions, experience, and faith. We are being resistant by not accepting simple answers, including just saying, "Well, there can be no God." Instead, we ask again, "Do I believe? Why do I believe? What do I believe?" In that moment, I accepted God's grace all over again. I confessed that I do believe in the resurrection; I am not to be pitied, because I share with my son in God's eternal kingdom.

That chapter in 1 Corinthians is an extended message of encouragement, particularly for those of us in that moment of doubt, depression, and just weariness. Paul reminds us that Christ died for our sins "and that he was buried, and that he was raised on the third day in accordance with the scriptures" (1 Cor. 15:4). Further, he assures us that just as Christ has been raised, so shall we. It is our creed; it is our confession. Paul's audience, however, was no different from us in that they couldn't help but wonder how such a thing is possible. After all, the entirety of human experience has taught us that once someone is dead, they are gone. They do not come back. "But someone will ask, 'How are the dead raised? With what kind of body do they come?'" (1 Cor. 15:35). What I love about Paul's response is not his flippancy (he calls the questioner a "fool"—Jesus had something to say about that [Matt. 5:22]), but the way in which he answers the question while seeming to dismiss it. Again, we do not get the mechanical details of what happens when we die, how it occurs, or even any clear idea of when we will be raised. Paul does, however, say that our raised bodies will be spiritual bodies—imperishable and immortal.

The image of our current bodies as seeds that, when planted, will give birth to spiritual bodies of power and glory has been on my mind of late. In the last few years of my father's life, the strokes and related issues he suffered left him thinner than usual, needing a walker, and having difficulty speaking—nothing too surprising for someone in his early eighties, but exacerbated by his illness. As I stood by his body with my mother and brother, he seemed so frail. "What is sown is perishable, what is raised is imperishable." It seemed in some way fitting that although he had been six feet two inches tall, an engineer, and witty in his prime, he now resembled the "seed" that was to be sown.

Think of a grain of wheat, as Paul suggests. It is so tiny, and yet it grows thousands of times in size and complexity when it is fully formed as the plant. The human being is amazingly complex and gorgeous as an organism. Not just the physical being, which is stunning enough, but consider our very nature, the mix of physical, psychological, emotional, and spiritual that combines into something so spectacularly unique that there are *never* any two alike. In the course of all existence, there have never been two humans that are the same. Even when there are "identical" twins (or more), they are never completely identical. And *that* is the seed. This incredibly complex and stunningly unique organism that each of us is will be the "simple" seed that will be resurrected into the unimaginably complex and beautiful spiritual body of glory and power. Just meditate on that for a bit. Let your mind wander. What might that be like? What might *we* be like in the World to Come? What will this meager seed, which is mighty and gracious already, be transformed into? It is pure speculation, of course, but I have found it humbling and encouraging to contemplate.

A wonderfully apt analogy came from a childhood friend of mine whose son had died almost a year before Mack. After Logan was diagnosed with a brain tumor, he battled with cancer for eighteen months before his body succumbed to the disease. Logan loved all things cars, including the Pixar movie *Cars*. Already by the age of three, Logan could identify the make of a car just from seeing its back corner. So each year on his birthday, his mom, Sherry, picks up a toy car (he particularly liked Corvettes and cars with flames painted on them) and puts it on his grave. This year she wrote about a small bit of grace that occurred as she was driving from the store after picking up some new cars that she knew he would like:

> As I drove down the road toward the house a minute later, "Life Is a Highway"—the theme to the original *Cars* movie—came on the radio. I was initially disappointed that it wasn't the Rascal Flatts version that played during the movie, but then I had a thought: sure, it's a different version, but it's still the same song with the same words and the same melody. And somehow, that truth made not knowing who Logan would be today a little less painful. It's like he was saying "it's still the same song, mom, just like I'm still me." Different, yes, but still with the same basic underpinnings that made him who he was (and still is).[2]

What a wonderful analogy! The melody remains, the essence is still the same, she recognized the song immediately, just as we will recognize our boys immediately. And yet they are so much *more* now than they were while here on the first earth. We are now the basic melody played out on the keyboard, but then we shall be a full orchestration! We will all be so much more.

Where and When

Over the millennia there have been any number of imaginations of the World to Come. Most people's imaginings come from the apocalyptic visions in Daniel and Revelation, with God on his throne pronouncing judgment, and angels waiting upon him and making declarations. There we also find the pearly gates and the roads paved with gold, God as an old man with white hair, and images of angels all around the throne singing God's praise. Inevitably, such images reveal much about the culture and community that developed them and their conception of God and heaven, but they do not tell us much about life after the resurrection because they are primarily concerned with the moment of judgment, not the time that follows. The Bible is not particularly verbose regarding the "new heaven and new earth," the world in which we will spend eternity.

In fact, the one place we find some clear statement, albeit still within the metaphorical language of apocalyptic literature, is in the next-to-last chapter of Revelation. In his vision John sees a "new heaven and a new earth; for the first heaven and the first earth had passed away" (Rev. 21:1). We will not, according to this vision, spend eternity in some cloudy, otherworldly heaven, but on the new earth, and God will reside with us: "See, the home of God is among mortals. He will dwell with them; they will be his peoples, and God himself will be with them" (21:3). The images of God walking in the garden with the man and the woman should spring to our minds as everything is being redeemed, transformed into God's original intention for creation. This is the reason for the emphasis upon God's judgment. It is not because God is vindictive, but because removing evil is necessary for the establishment of the holy and good creation. We, humanity, have exerted our free will, we have acted upon our impulses, we have repented and returned to God, and now "he will wipe every tear from our eyes." Evil, in reality and in all its metaphorical expressions, will be destroyed, removed from existence so that "death will be no more, mourning and crying and pain will be no more, for the first things have passed away" (21:4). And God and humanity will again walk in the garden together, in communion with one another. This is the "new heaven and new earth" that John sees in his revelation, and we talk about this as being at the end of time.

It is understandable that we wonder, and in some cases worry, about what happens in between, after we die and before Jesus returns and unites heaven and earth. This was a question and concern from the beginning of the church, and so Paul writes, "We do not want you to be uninformed, brothers and sisters, about those who have died, so that you may not grieve as others do who have no hope" (1 Thess. 4:13). It is natural that we seek assurances and make speculations. In medieval stories, we read accounts of righteous men and women seeing Jesus and a host of saints receiving them in their last moments. Today we often encourage one another, without much thought behind it, by saying that our loved ones are now "with Jesus in heaven." There are numerous speculations about what happens at death. N. T. Wright has written extensively on this subject, offering a good corrective to the various nonbiblical understandings of the resurrection.[3] In particular, Wright emphasizes the fact that the Bible describes our *physical* resurrection and ultimately the union of heaven and earth, where we will begin this new "life *after* life after death."[4] He also argues from Paul's description of the dead as being "asleep" that we will enter an "intermediate state," one in which we are with God and with Christ yet are not yet resurrected.[5] This image of "restful happiness" is certainly consistent with Scripture and more in line with its testimony than the fluffy clouds of popular Christian culture, yet he admits that it is often not a very comforting image for those whose loved ones have died.[6]

The idea that they are simply in a kind of stasis—as opposed to being immediately with Christ in their new resurrection bodies—can be very disheartening to some who mourn, no matter the ultimate joy of the resurrection. I have spoken with many who find the image of their loved one, and eventually themselves, being in some sort of spiritual coma very disconcerting. While Wright finds this consistent with Scripture and for him it is a picture of complete peace, others find greater comfort in knowing that their loved one is already transformed and watching over them. In light of that, I want to encourage you to hold on to the conception of what happens after we die that brings *you* comfort and strength. All such speculation is just that, speculation based upon general imagery in the Bible that is intended to provide comfort and encouragement to the faithful. Paul uses the image of those who have died in Christ being "asleep," but it is just a metaphor; he does not articulate that as a doctrine as he has done with the actual, bodily resurrection (1 Cor. 15). So if Wright's description or my own theorizing in the following section does not provide you comfort, just set it aside. The only purpose is to offer comfort and consolation in the truth of the resurrection.

Immediate Resurrection

Years ago, long before I began serious theological study, I wrestled with this question of what happens to us when we die. I came to a different understanding from Wright's that I do not believe is in conflict with Scripture, but I

readily admit that is not clearly stated. During my sopho-
more year at Cornell, I clearly remember sitting by Beebe
Lake, in the old sandwich shop called the "Noyes Lodge,"
thinking about the fact that so much time had elapsed since
Jesus ascended "to prepare a place for us" that Abraham
was closer to the time of Jesus than we are.[7] How do we
reconcile the extreme length of time that has elapsed with
the promise of the Parousia—Jesus' return to bring justice and healing, mercy and grace? What is he waiting for?
God knows (literally) we need it!

All those years ago, the thought occurred to me that
God is outside of time. After all, God has always been and
so existed before the conception of time. That being the
case, why must we continue to think of "life after death"
in a linear progression? Of course, we live in a historical
"line," with one moment occurring after another, day after
day, and so we tell our stories in a linear fashion; the Bible
does likewise. Yet if we recognize that God is outside of
time and space, could it not be that when one dies one is
also outside of this linear path? If so, regardless of the point
in history at which we each die, we all arise at the same
moment, on the Day of the Resurrection. Christ's return,
then, is not delayed but is always in the future and always
at this moment.

These are the thoughts that occurred to me when I
was twenty. Over the years, I have shared my speculation
with others in Sunday school classes and in an essay on
my website. After Mack died, I returned to this possibility
and reshared that essay on the site, pointing out that I find
comfort in the thought that my grandfather, Mack, and I
will all open our eyes in the World to Come at the same
time. Mack is not "waiting" for me, Elizabeth, or Jesus; we
all arrive at the end of this world and the beginning of the
next right on time at the same time. A commenter asked if I
was informed by the work of Emil Brunner. I had to admit
I had never heard of the outstanding Swiss theologian. I
had not heard of him when I was twenty or even late into

my forties. It is perhaps not surprising that I (and others) had not heard of Brunner, since he is often (and was in his own lifetime) overshadowed by his contemporary Karl Barth, but I have since read much of what he wrote, and he is deserving of study.[8]

The Brunner work that is most relevant here is *Eternal Hope*, and I was not terribly surprised when I found that this work was dedicated to his deceased sons Peter and Thomas. Brunner, it turns out, had long ago observed that God is, indeed, outside of our spheres of time and space and that as such, our conceptions of life being made up of discrete, linear moments is misleading: "The being with Christ is not the moment immediately after death. *For in the eternal world there is no next moment.* In death the world of space and time disappears, and . . . the being with Christ and the future coming of the Lord [are] both . . . one and the same."[9] What Brunner is expressing (and the idea in the first sentence that we are not "with Christ" at the moment immediately after death may sound heretical or discomforting) is that this conception of linear time—that we move from one moment, "alive," to another moment, "dead on earth, but alive with Christ"—is nonexistent once we are no longer tied to this world. As he says, being with Christ and the Parousia, the future coming of the Lord, are one and the same.

Of course, it all depends upon the perspective from which one perceives it, our temporal plane or the eternal. Brunner says earlier, "So also the departing and being with Christ is no merely individual personal happening but only the this-worldly appearance of what from the other-worldly angle is called the Parousia."[10] So what we often consider a specific future moment within this timeline of history, a fixed point albeit unknown to humanity, is from the perspective of God the moment when each individual dies, since at that same moment all have died.

Once we set aside our linear view of time, our vision expands and there is no longer meaning to the sequencing of "moments." Moments, from the eternal perspective, are simply "now." That also opens up a broader understanding of God's sovereignty, agency, and omniscience. From the eternal, all can be seen and known, but that does not mean that it is directed or ordained in a mechanistic sense. God is sovereign and knows all our days, but that does not mean that God has dictated all evil and suffering that befalls us in this life.

Is this conception of the moment of death being the moment of Parousia accurate? No one can know. It is a conception, a depiction, an attempt to understand, to the best of our knowledge on this temporal plane, what happens when we move from this world to the next. The New Testament has other images, but they all are efforts to express the ultimately ineffable and, in so doing, to provide comfort and encouragement to us now, in *this* moment. Take such comfort as you find in these imaginations, but set aside that which does not draw you closer to Christ and his peace.

What we know is the promise of the resurrection, our eternal life in Christ, though the mechanism of this is unknown. Brunner concludes his chapter in just this way: "*Summa summarum*: We know nothing of the how, we know only the fact, and its implication: that it will be the end of history in the Kingdom of God, the judgment and the perfecting of creation in the eternal world."[11] Amen.

Alleluia.
Christ our Passover lamb has been sacrificed for us;
therefore let us keep the feast,
Not with the old leaven, the leaven of malice and evil,
but with the unleavened bread of sincerity and truth. Alleluia.

Christ being raised from the dead will never die again;
death no longer has dominion over him.
The death that he died, he died to sin, once for all;

but the life he lives, he lives to God.
So also consider yourselves dead to sin,
and alive to God in Jesus Christ our Lord. Alleluia.

Christ has been raised from the dead,
the first fruits of those who have fallen asleep.
For since by a man came death,
by a man has come also the resurrection of the dead.
For as in Adam all die,
so also in Christ shall all be made alive. Alleluia.[12]

Reflection Questions

1. Do you have a clear picture of heaven? Where did that image come from? Does it bring you comfort when reflecting on loved ones' deaths or your own?
2. Read 1 Corinthians 15:12–28. How does your belief in the resurrection of Christ influence the way you think about life after death? How does the idea of Christ's second coming influence the way you think about life after death?
3. What do you think happens after we die? How do you feel about the idea of being "asleep" until a future resurrection?
4. How do you envision your loved one's after-death existence or experience? Are there elements of that vision that you find particularly comforting or powerful?
5. Does the idea of God and God's kingdom being outside of time transform your thinking about the resurrection and the afterlife as we experience it?

CHAPTER 9

THE ALREADY
AND THE NOT YET

We know the end of the story. And we experience the beautiful and terrible things of this life. But how do we live in between the already and the not yet? We have discussed the pragmatic steps we might take to keep walking, to live in grace, and to move forward from a point of tragedy. Keeping busy, however, only gets us so far. Seeking to live fully, we walk on in faith and with the conviction of our resurrection into eternal life in the kingdom of God. Paul looked to the end of history and decided that "the sufferings of this present time are not worth comparing with the glory about to be revealed to us" (Rom. 8:18). Keeping in view the joyous end enabled Paul to endure what were clearly horrific events. My father grew up on a ranch in south central Texas, and he used to tell me how he had learned to be able to walk across the pasture where the cattle were grazing, keeping his eyes up, scanning the horizon for his destination, while not stepping in a single cowpat. He said the key was to know your destination but be aware of your surroundings. Although a bit scatological, this is not a bad analogy for making your way through life, cow patties and all.

In order to make our way through this world, whether it be a particular moment or the grand sweep of life, we need the three pillars of spiritual strength: "And now faith, hope, and love abide, these three; and the greatest of these is love" (1 Cor. 13:13). Paul is writing in the oft-quoted 1 Corinthians 13 about all the ways in which love is an action, something we do. (I always point out in weddings that Jesus and Paul call us to love one another. They never say anything about liking each other. Fondness is fleeting, but love is a commitment to care.) While the greatest may be love, it is faith and hope that complete the three legs needed for a stable foundation. We act in faith, based upon our hope of the resurrection, and that provides us with the freedom and confidence to be vulnerable, to risk being hurt, so that we can love others in the here and now. It is the destination on the horizon that we must keep in clear view in our mind's eye. This is how we live in between, but it requires our resolve.

While I was next to Mack in the hospital in his final hours, I read to him from *The Hobbit*. We had just finished reading it together at bedtime a few weeks earlier, and I thought it might reassure him to hear my voice—and it allowed me to do *something*. After he died, I decided to reread all of The Lord of the Rings novels. An exchange between Frodo and Gandalf struck me as a nice summation of where we all find ourselves in this world. The hobbit Frodo has been tasked with destroying the ring of power, and as dark forces chase him and seek to overwhelm the whole world, Frodo expresses his dismay that it should have to happen to him, that it had to happen now.

"I wish it need not have happened in my time," said Frodo.

"So do I," said Gandalf, "and so do all who live to see such times. But that is not for them to decide. All we have to decide is what to do with the time that is given us."[1]

Tolkien was moved and inspired in his writings by his experience in the trenches of World War I and as a witness to World War II. It seemed as if the entire globe was going to be consumed in hate and war. "There will be wars and rumors of wars," as Jesus says. The sad truth is that we all live in such times, all the time.

In the weeks that follow any death, but especially that of a young person who leaves us so unexpectedly like Mack or Ashley, there is hardly any time for reflection. We may feel that we have no agency, there are no choices left for us to make that are worthwhile. I remember when we met with the funeral home director to plan the arrangements for Mack's viewing and funeral and to pick out a coffin. Even when it came to the coffin, we had no choice. They had only one for a child of Mack's size, a white metal coffin. (I still regret not allowing Mack's buddies to decorate it with spray paint. I think it would have been therapeutic for all of us and that Mack would have thought it was hilarious.)[2] It is understandable that we feel helpless and defeated when these sorts of tragedies come upon us.

The most devastating aspect to our own recovery is perhaps the sense that there is nothing we can do, that there is no way to change the reality that we now live in. I cannot tell you how often we still say to one another, "I can't believe that Mack is gone." But while we cannot alter the past that has brought us to our new, painful present, we *do* still have agency. When that realization comes upon us it can, in fact, be clarifying and liberating. Yes, this is the world we live in; it has always had death and suffering, which we now experience in a more personal way, and it hurts like hell. Whatever illusions we had in the past, now we have to confront the fact that there is sin and suffering in this world. But with that honest assessment of life also comes a deeper understanding of what Jesus did for humanity and the world on the cross and the completion of his work through his resurrection.

We cannot control the hurtfulness of the world, but we can make our own choices about what we do in the next moment. To paraphrase Gandalf, what remains to us is to decide what we are going to do with the time, and the grace, that has been given to us. On that last night, after Mack had died, Elizabeth and I asked each other how we could go on. The answer was in faith, hope, and love. Of course, we didn't articulate it in those terms. We believed that Mack was now more alive and healthier than he would ever have been in this world and that we would someday join him. We also knew that our love for him, for Izzy, and for one another did not stop at death.

Inhabiting Our Exile

We live daily, then, in this tension of the "already and the not yet." Christ has already won the victory and has given us eternal life through his sacrifice. God will restore all creation to its intended glory and ourselves to his divine image—but not yet. In the meantime, we have to continue to live in this beautiful and terrible world, with the hope of the resurrection and the reality of hunger and sickness. We live in between. We are constantly in transition, never quite arriving at our intended destination. These moments of transition are expressed all the time in life, even if we only mark them occasionally. It is most obvious at funerals, but we feel it as well when we cross the stage at graduation, walk down the aisle at our wedding, drive the car cross-country to our first job, or liquidate our assets to prepare for retirement. We are always living in between. We live, in other words, in exile.

The Babylonian king Nebuchadnezzar laid siege to and conquered Jerusalem in 586 BCE, the event commemorated

in the book of Lamentations. After the conquest, the Baby-
lonians took the royalty, priests, and leaders of Judah into
exile in Babylon. The prophet Jeremiah lived through
this entire period, preaching both God's punishment upon
Israel and the promise of God's grace and succor. You can
imagine how restless and anxious those living in exile in
Babylon must have been. They wanted to return to their
homeland. They grieved those who had been killed, they
were suffering in a strange land, and they just wanted to
go back home. God's message to them was unexpected and
simple: sit tight. "Build houses and live in them; plant gar-
dens and eat what they produce. Take wives and have sons
and daughters; take wives for your sons, and give your
daughters in marriage, that they may bear sons and daughters; multiply there, and do not decrease" (Jer. 29:5–6).
God was telling them that they were going to be in Babylon for a while and that they should settle down and make
the best of it. They were to make the best of it, but they
were not to be idle. God also told them to "seek the welfare of the city where I have sent you into exile, and pray
to the LORD on its behalf, for in its welfare you will find
your welfare" (Jer. 29:7). Settle down in Babylon, build
your homes and families, and care for the people around
you—the same people who conquered you, killed your
families, and sent you into exile in the first place. Pray for
their welfare, for it is your own. The people were to inhabit
their exile. That meant living in the moment, being God's
presence in Babylon, even as they waited and trusted in
God's promise that they would return to Jerusalem. In the
meantime, they had the work of God to do right where
they were.

Right where we are is right where God is. The fantasti-
cal imagery of Ezekiel's vision of God's throne was another
message of encouragement sent to the Jews living in Babylon. This vision with which the book of Ezekiel opens is
called the *Merkavah,* or "throne" in Hebrew (from which
Merkavah mysticism in Judaism takes its name), and it

is given to Ezekiel in exile by the river Chebar. He sees a great wind coming out of the north, and in its midst is flashing fire and "something like gleaming amber."[3] There are four amazing creatures, each with four faces, four hands, and four wings: "Their wings touched one another; each of them moved straight ahead, without turning as they moved" (Ezek. 1:9). Further, each has a wheel by its side. "*Wherever* the spirit would go, they went, and the wheels rose along with them; for the spirit of the living creatures was in the wheels" (v. 20, emphasis mine).

What is the point of this amazing vision of the "throne chariot" of God? It is a vital message that seems obvious to us today but was far from assumed in sixth-century BCE Judah: God is not bound to one location. There is no place where God's people can go that the Lord God is not also present. Even in exile, God is still with his people. Remember, the temple of Jerusalem had been destroyed. That was "God's footstool," the place where the law said sacrifices must be offered on a daily basis. The destruction of Jerusalem was devastating and no doubt caused many to question whether or not the Lord was still their god, because it seemed like Marduk, the god of Babylon, had, in fact, bested him on his own turf. Then the vision came to Ezekiel on the banks of the river Chebar to tell those living in exile, "I am with you." There is nowhere that we can go where God is not.

We too live in exile. Our ultimate home is in the new heaven and new earth that is yet to come (at least from our historical perspective); in the meantime, we are to build up our families and homes while caring for those around us. And God is here with us, in this place.

"I Will Be with You Always"

I now view Holy Saturday in a completely different way since Mack died. I understand better the devastation of the disciples and their absolute befuddlement on that day after

Jesus was cruelly crucified and before the risen Christ had appeared to the women. I am certain that they felt God had abandoned them, that God was *not* with them at that moment. I am certain because I know, in a deeply personal way, the despair and despondency that come from a loved one being dragged from you. They just sat in that room, not knowing what to do next or where to go. It was shock. It was grief. In many ways, we all live in a constant Holy Saturday. We live in the moment of the pain of this world, and while Jesus made promises of coming again (the disciples can certainly be forgiven for not realizing what Jesus meant when he said, "Destroy this temple, and in three days I will raise it up"), we struggle to move to the next moment of living. It can seem that we live between Good Friday and Easter Sunday. In fact, on more than one Easter weekend, I have preached just that message, that every day for us is Holy Saturday. But I now believe that is not true and was the wrong message.

We leave in a post-Easter world. On that day after Jesus was killed, the disciples were fearful and uncertain. They were paralyzed, uncertain what to do or even what to think of all that had just happened. But then Jesus burst into that room and back into their lives, this time in a way that transcended his mere personal presence. He was with them again—until he was gone again. But before he left, Jesus said, "I am with you always, to the end of the age" (Matt. 28:20). Living *after* Easter meant that Jesus would never again be apart from us, or us from Jesus. Now "Christ is all and in all!" (Col. 3:11). Jesus ascended into heaven and yet remains with us in a very real and present way.

The world has forever been transformed. We will all still endure the sort of fear, doubt, and uncertainty of Holy Saturday, but we know that Jesus has been raised from the dead, and that he is just the first. This is the foundation of our faith, the promise of Jesus that was confirmed by his resurrection and sealed in his ascension. The author of Hebrews has a wonderful phrase to express the certainty of the promises of God: "This hope [is] a sure and steadfast anchor of the soul" (Heb. 6:19). As we say together in the eucharistic prayer, "Christ has died, Christ is risen, Christ *will* come again." That is the anchor of our soul, the foundation of our faith, and from that position of strength and security we can continue to live in this beautiful and terrible world of the already and the not yet.

That is our faith and hope, but that doesn't mean it's easy. Over the millennia Christians have learned to live with the fact that the Parousia has not yet come (at least not in our linear framework of history). Or perhaps it has just become impersonal to us; we don't feel it the way the people who lived with and loved Jesus did. So long as it remains a theological abstraction, we seem able to cope. But when our own beloved is taken from us, that challenge of continuing to live in this world while being assured of the world to come becomes poignant, even painful. Theologically, the truth is the truth, and we shouldn't require our own loss for it to become "real" to us. Yet it often does. The promise of the resurrection remains as valid as ever, but we cannot deny that it is even more relevant to those of us who yearn to be reunited with our loved ones in the world to come.

Now, more than ever, we lean into the promises of God. We lament and rail against God in our grief and bitterness, but we also praise God and declare, "Your mercies are new every morning." Because no matter where we go, no matter how dark the valley of our mind, no matter how deep our depression, God is there with us, loving us. God first loved us, not only so that we might love others, but so that we could love ourselves (1 John 4:19). This is how God turns mourning into dancing: he gives us his grace, his love for us, and calls us to love and care for everyone, ourselves included. The full and ultimate elimination of all evil, death, and suffering is not yet here, but in the meantime, we have work to do—the work of the kingdom of God.

The Kingdom of God

When I think of the kingdom of God, a line from another U2 song always pops into mind. In the title track on the 1981 album *October*, Bono sings about kingdoms rising and falling, impermanent as the falling leaves in October. Bono was asked about the song and the album in a 1982 interview in Hattem, Netherlands.[4] "October," he said, "is an image. We've been through the '60s, we've been through a time where things were in full bloom. . . . Everybody thought how great mankind was. And now, as you go through the '70s and the '80s, it's a colder time of year; it's after the harvest, the trees are stripped bare, and you can see things. We've finally realized, maybe we weren't so smart after all." Almost forty years since that album was released, the sentiment remains — kingdoms are built and they crumble, "but you go on." Who is "you"? I don't know who Bono might have had in mind, although given other U2 songs from that album and era, I would not be surprised if it was God.

The notion of "kings" and "kingdoms" is not unproblematic, and today we find many people shying away from using such terms for God and the community of the faithful. The reason is simple: most kings and kingdoms at some point become corrupt. Even David, "the man after God's own heart," was an adulterer and a murderer. Yet as Jesus was living in a region ruled by despotic leaders, he still used these images of kingdom to describe the work of the Holy Spirit in the world and the day of God's restoration of creation.

If you do a search of the Gospels for the phrase "kingdom of God" and the more-or-less interchangeable phrase "kingdom of heaven," you will find that Jesus uses these terms in what seem to be two distinct and seemingly contradictory ways. Often the kingdom of God is described as the work of the Spirit in the world today, such as in the parable of the Sower or of the Mustard Seed in Mark 4. The farmer does not know how the seed grows but plants it and nurtures it, and it grows to yield its fruit. The mustard seed is so small, yet it grows into a bush so large "that the birds of the air can make nests in its shade" (v. 32). The kingdom of God was also already present in some way, since Jesus tells the Pharisees in Luke 17:21 that it is already among them, albeit unseen. When demons are being cast out, it is because the kingdom of God has already arrived (Matt. 12:28).

More often, "the kingdom of God" or "the kingdom of heaven" is used to refer to the establishment of God's rule and order, the Day of the Lord, and the life within God's eternal kingdom that will follow. So it is described as being near or "at hand" when people are called to repentance. Jesus declared, "The time is fulfilled, and the kingdom of God has come near; repent, and believe in the good news" (Mark 1:15). The kingdom of heaven is also like a great banquet, an image we often evoke in calling people to the "Lord's Table" for Communion, while forgetting that the master of the banquet threw some out of the party (Matt. 22). The wealthy and those who are overly concerned with the things of this world will struggle to enter the kingdom of heaven, but for those who seek the kingdom of heaven, "all these things will be given to you as well" (Matt 6:33). The kingdom of God is all these things; it is the already and the not yet. While we are not the host of the banquet, we are the servants who are tasked with inviting the guests. We are the gardeners planting seeds, tending vines, and preparing the harvest. The Spirit works through us to grow the kingdom of God.

God's Word, both the message of the Gospel and the Word made flesh, is planted within us and is to be shared, scattered throughout the world. Often we may not see it growing, taking shape as it germinates, but it is at work, nonetheless, and it yields fruit. At the harvest, the fruit of the kingdom of God will be justice and judgment. If a human kingdom is supposed to bring justice, how much more so God's kingdom? Yet in the meantime, that kingdom grows as a sheltering plant, offering nourishment, protection, and strength to all who seek shelter in its branches. We, the church, are both the mustard tree and those seeking shelter within it.

Meanwhile, we live in between, after the planting of the seed but before the harvest. Kingdoms rise and kingdoms fall, but we are to go on. This is the work that Christians are called to do in between. The way in which we move from our place of grief is to find purpose and meaning in our walk. While the specifics are left for the individual to prayerfully discern, Jesus has provided our primary purpose in calling us to inhabit our exile. So long as it is "now," and so long as we live in this world, we are to make it our home. That means, among other things, that we are to love and pray for those around us, even those who have perhaps harmed us deeply and grievously. It also means that we receive the gift and grace of God working through others in our lives. We find life after death in living out the gospel.

When Jesus ascended into heaven, he told the disciples that he would always be with them. God sent the Holy Spirit to be our advocate and comforter to dwell in us and be with us (John 14:17). Even when it feels that there is no one else around, no one who can relate to our heartache or pain, the Spirit of God is with us. Often we find God working through the people around us, and just as we may find life and joy in helping others, we also need to recognize and receive the blessings that are being offered to us.

In Luke's Gospel, just before Jesus says, "In fact, the kingdom of God is among you," there is a curious story of a group of lepers being healed by Jesus (Luke 17:11–19). These ten lepers see Jesus, and keeping their distance, they call out "Jesus, Master, have mercy on us!" Jesus does not reply by saying "You are healed" or "Be well," but, curiously, "Go and show yourselves to the priests." He says this because according to biblical law (Lev. 14), once a person with leprosy has been healed and cleansed, that person is supposed to go to the priests for confirmation.

But you only go to the priests *once you have been healed*. Unlike other episodes of healing, Jesus does not say that they are healed or their sins are forgiven; he simply tells them to go to the priests.

Luke describes the scene: "And as they went, they were made clean. Then one of them, when he saw that he was healed, turned back, praising God with a loud voice. He prostrated himself at Jesus' feet and thanked him. And he was a Samaritan" (Luke 17:14b–16). I can't tell you why the others did not come back and praise God. I suspect it's because they did not realize it had happened. How many other rabbis might have told them, "Get the priest to look at it," in hopes that this time the disease might have subsided? The words of Jesus might have seemed perfunctory to them, a brush off. It is impossible to know what they were thinking and why they didn't notice, but as they walked along the way, the Samaritan *did* look, and he noticed that he had been healed, and he gave glory to God for his healing.

The Samaritan offers us an example of how to live as we walk between two worlds. We live in exile, moving ever toward that return and restoration God has promised us in Christ Jesus. But as we walk along this difficult, dark path, do we notice the healing that God has *already* provided us in our lives? At any point in our life we may feel hurt and alone. Our suffering may seem beyond all comforting. Yet Jesus is always with us, and he suffered as we have suffered so that he can be our comforter and advocate. The cleansing and healing of Jesus' work in our lives has already begun if we are willing to notice our blessings and give thanks.

O God, Creator of heaven and earth: Grant that, as the crucified body of your dear Son was laid in the tomb and rested on that holy Sabbath, so we may await with him the coming of the third day, and rise with him to newness of life; who now lives and reigns with you and the Holy Spirit, one God, for ever and ever. Amen.[5]

Reflection Questions

1. How does taking a long view of God's story help you navigate the difficult times of the here and now?
2. Reflect on the time you find yourself in, and then, as Gandalf advised, consider what you can do with the time that you have and make a list of the positive things you can do.
3. Read Jeremiah 29:5–7. Imagine hearing these instructions for yourself. What does it mean for you to "settle down" and seek the welfare of the community you find yourself in?
4. Do you feel like you are living in a prolonged Holy Saturday? How does it feel to remind yourself that while there is still darkness in this world, Christ is also already resurrected?
5. The full establishment of the kingdom of God will only be done by God, but in many ways it is already here, and we are part of building that kingdom. How does the knowledge of the future kingdom of God encourage you? What role do you feel called to play now in the building of the kingdom here and now?

CHAPTER 10

HOPE

As my mother and I sat by my father's bed in the ICU, we began to talk about plans for his funeral—not immediately, but after a day or so, when it became clear that his perishable body was ready to yield to the imperishable. Mom said she knew Dad wanted a service like Mack's. She said they both loved how it was focused not upon the deceased, but on the resurrection of Jesus. Ever since my father had given his life to Christ as a teenager, his devout wish was to share the gospel with others so that they might know Jesus as he did, as their Lord and Savior. This was so much a part of his being that in an earlier hospital visit, while they thought he was asleep, Dad suddenly awoke, looked at the nurse checking his IV and croaked, "Do you know Jesus?" He was a gentle man in his witnessing. He wouldn't tell you that you were going to hell, but he did want you to know Jesus as he did, he wanted you to join him in eternal life. And that was what he wanted at his funeral service—not an encomium about his life, but the declaration of Christ crucified and risen from the dead.

This is the hope of the resurrection—the firm conviction and sure promise that just as Jesus was raised from the dead, so too will we. I was raised in a large, evangelical Presbyterian church, and the Episcopal service that Mom and Dad had so liked was new to them; it was simply "The Burial of the Dead" from *The Book of Common Prayer*. It begins with the proclamation, "I am the Resurrection and I am the Life, says the Lord. Whoever has faith in me shall have life, even though they die. And everyone who has life, and has committed themselves to me in faith, shall not die for ever" (John 11:25–26). In many ways, it is like all the other services in the Anglican tradition and found in *The Book of Common Prayer*. The reading of Scripture and the proclamation of the Gospel are at the heart of the service, followed by the congregation's affirming the Christian faith in the words of the creed (in this case, the Apostles' Creed) and then praying together and responsively. The Eucharist, or Communion, may be included, as we did at Mack's service, and that further draws the community together around the sacrifice of Jesus that has transformed *this* death from an ending of life into the beginning of the new, eternal spiritual life. For as Paul wrote, and is read in the service, "What is sown is perishable, what is raised is imperishable. . . . It is sown a physical body, it is raised a spiritual body" (1 Cor. 15:42, 44). This is the hope that my father believed fervently, it is at the heart of the gospel, and it is the promise that God has made to all creation through Jesus. It has brought me great comfort, but I admit it is not always easy to hold on to hope.

The Challenge of Hope

Shortly after Mack died, a colleague from the university came by my office. She was a development officer, the mother of one of my students, and a member of our parish. She brought with her two identical, small, framed quotes from Sister Joan Chittister—one for me and one for my wife. At the time, I had no idea who Joan Chittister was. Now I know her writings (although not as well as my wife, who is a devoted reader of her works) and have come to appreciate everything from her commitment to the Catholic Church and its reform (whether the leadership wants it or not) to her thoughtful, spiritual, contemplative writings. The framed gift given to us within weeks of Mack's death had a simple drawing of a heart, whole yet with lines through it like stained glass, and a short quote that was direct and to the point: "Hope is the ability to believe that good can happen out of anything." The sense of the quote is to encourage us that no matter how difficult things become, there is the possibility of redemption. Something good can yet emerge out of the darkness.

Paul offers us those three pillars of spiritual strength—faith, hope, and love—and while he says that love is the greatest of the three, it is in hope through faith that we are able to love. When we are at our lowest, even when we are unable to love ourselves let alone someone else, it is hope that gives us the strength to move forward. That is the truth in Sister Joan's statement, and it moves us beyond Paul's reflection that this current suffering is nothing compared to the joy we will experience. Sister Joan is encouraging us to see that while we cannot change the past or how we got to this present moment, we know that God is with us as we choose to move forward and that God will redeem the experience. We operate then in the hope of the future work of God in our lives as we acknowledge God's current presence, his entering into our own history, and as we affirm that the Holy Spirit is at work in our lives.

There is perhaps no word with greater ambiguity and yet more discussion of its meaning than *hope*. In everyday parlance, it can carry the sense of wishful thinking, a desire for some outcome or something to be true without any evidence that it ought to be true. That notion is not new, and for many, hope is simply fantasy—baseless positive, personal psychology. Throughout history, some have thought of hope as an evil that causes people to refuse to acknowledge the harsh reality of life.

The story of Pandora is an ancient theodicy, an attempt to explain evil and suffering in this world. The ancient Greek poet Hesiod recounts how after Prometheus stole fire and gave it to men (not humanity, as there were only men at this point), Zeus wanted to punish men and so ordered Pandora to be created out of the earth, the first woman. Pandora brought with her a jar (often mistranslated as "box") that contained all manner of pain, disease, evil, and hope. When the jar was opened, all of these flew out except hope: "Hope alone remained within the unbreakable house beneath the lip of the jar, and did not fly out the door."[1] Thus evil entered the world—but not hope. There remains debate to this day as to whether the fact that hope remains in the jar is a mercy or further punishment. Some in antiquity thought that hope was an evil. It draws one away from actually living, engaging in the present, real world. Philosophers throughout history have taken similar views. Although Nietzsche softened his position with age, his earlier statement represents a significant stream of thought: "Zeus did not wish man, however much he might be tormented by the other evils, to fling away his life, but to go on letting himself be tormented again and again. Therefore he gives Man hope, in reality it is the worst of all evils, because it prolongs the torments of Man."[2] That is the evil many see in hope; it provides unwarranted expectations that life may get better and thus prolongs our torment in this life.

That is not the biblical view of hope. Hope is, of course, always a looking forward, an expectation of something that has not yet happened. In the biblical context, it is looking forward to the Day of the Lord, the resurrection, and the re-creation of all things. The hope of Christianity, however, is not a baseless, unwarranted expectation. It is grounded in the witness of the resurrection of Jesus and the promises of God. It is the testimony of others who have called out to God and felt the presence of the Holy Spirit in their lives and seen God's power at work, transforming the darkness into light, bringing good out of anything. It is upon that basis that we hope, and in the words of the Nicene Creed, "look for the resurrection of the dead and the life of the world to come."

Yet living in the hope of the resurrection is not escapism. Christians and Christianity acknowledge fully the hurting and hurtful nature of this world. In Paul's great passage on hope, Romans 8, he describes creation itself as groaning in anticipation of its redemption: "For the creation waits with eager longing for the revealing of the children of God . . . in hope that the creation itself will be set free from its bondage to decay and will obtain the freedom of the glory of the children of God" (vv. 19–21). The hope of the resurrection is the looking forward to when *all* creation, heaven and earth and humanity, will be transformed into the glory that God intended for us at the outset. Meanwhile, we continue to live in this world, even as we look and work with expectation for the world to come, in the sure hope of God's kingdom come.

No, hope is not escapism; it is essential. Brunner opens his study by observing the absolute necessity of hope for all humanity:

What oxygen is for the lungs, such is hope for the meaning of human life. Take oxygen away and death occurs through suffocation, take hope away and humanity is constricted through lack of breath; despair supervenes, spelling the paralysis of intellectual and spiritual powers by a feeling of the senselessness and purposelessness of existence. As the fate of the human organism is dependent on the supply of oxygen, so the fate of humanity is dependent on its supply of hope.[3]

Hopeful Lament

Hope is the very substance of the means of our existence and is at the heart of what might seem the most hopeless of expressions: the lament. I began this reflection by sharing my involuntary and inward cry of lament borrowed from the psalmist: "My God! Why have you forsaken me!" A declaration more than a question, it came from the depth of my soul; it was my honest, angry cry of tears and pain as I demanded to be heard by God. That lament, every lamentation, is the honest expression of our anger, fears, and expectations all founded upon hope. If I had no hope that God would hear me, why would I cry out? Why complain and call for God to comfort me? Yet in lament we express our hope for the future, based upon God's faithfulness in the past:

> In you our ancestors trusted;
>   they trusted, and you delivered them.
> To you they cried, and were saved;
>   in you they trusted, and were not put to shame.
> —Ps. 22:4–5

We look back in our own lives and remember when God was near, when we felt the love of God through the love of others and experienced the "coincidences" that were just what we needed in that time.

I readily admit that I am not someone who has had visions from God, nor have I felt a strong voice in my thoughts, directing me when I have been in a moment of strife or dismay. What I *have* experienced, and on many occasions, are amazing interruptions in my life that have shown me the Spirit of God at work. Shortly after graduating from college I had such a striking set of circumstances. I had been dating a woman for over three years, and we had begun to make plans to get married. I purchased a ring and traveled to the country where she was studying.

Before I could even show her the ring, let alone unpack my bags, she told me that our relationship would go no further. She was right, and I was grateful to her for her honesty and forthrightness. But I grieved. My prayers and plans had evaporated. Yet I also felt a peace. It *was* the right decision, and I don't know if I would have made it. She did.

I returned to my graduate program and decided to volunteer at the radio station. There, "coincidentally," was this remarkable woman who had recently returned from mission work in West Africa. Elizabeth had plans of her own that included serving God and *not* dating anyone. Fourteen months later we were married, and we have continued to experience God's presence through all sorts of wonderful, difficult, and demanding times, from the call the day before our wedding offering a chance to study at Oxford, England, to the hundreds of people who came to Mack's funeral. We entered into the union of heart, body, and mind intended by God for our "mutual joy and for the help and comfort given one another in prosperity and adversity" not knowing what might be ahead but certain of God's presence with us.[4] Our hope rests in God for today *and* tomorrow.

So we must remember the past and hope for the future even as we walk in the confidence of the love of God. It is never an easy journey, and it requires honesty. We must look truthfully at our own lives and the world we live in. Counter to young Nietzsche, hope does not keep us in a pliable state but rather provides us with the resilience and strength needed to be honest about life. When we hope, we can address wickedness and hurt in the confidence that God will ultimately bring justice and healing to all of creation. Through hope, we can come through joblessness and broken relationships and walk forward with purpose and meaning.

Honesty requires us also to acknowledge that we may struggle to find those moments of grace in our lives; they may be few and far between. We should be encouraged to remember that it was only on a very few moments that God spoke to Abraham. According to Genesis, during Abraham's long life, there seem to be decades when he heard nothing from God, even as he was obeying God's command to go to a new land. Yet in setting these moments side by side, a narrative emerges of God's presence in his life, God's direction and provision for Abraham and his family. Elizabeth and I have had moments when it felt that God was ordering our every step from one blessing to the next. Then we have had times when we felt our faithfulness has been for naught. Yet even then we have found God to be present. When we honestly assess our own lives, neither omitting the periods of wilderness nor the times of comfort, a narrative will emerge that includes both suffering and grace. In this world there are both beautiful and terrible things, and it is the knowledge that God is with us and the hope of life eternal that enable us to make our way. God says, "Don't be afraid. I am with you. Nothing can ever separate us. It's for you I created the universe. I love you."[5]

Live Today, in Peace

Paul fully recognizes the difficulty and challenges of this life. He knows that to persevere through the dark valleys requires reminding ourselves that in the midst of the suffering is also the grace of God:

Therefore, since we are justified by faith, we have peace with God through our Lord Jesus Christ, through whom we have obtained access to this grace in which we stand; and we boast in our hope of sharing the glory of God. And not only that, but we also boast in our sufferings, knowing that suffering produces endurance, and endurance produces character, and character produces hope, and hope does not disappoint us, because God's love has been poured into our hearts through the Holy Spirit that has been given to us. (Rom. 5:1–5)

This passage is often misused to justify our suffering, to argue that God has sent atrocities to us in order to build us up, but Paul is not addressing the origins of suffering at all. He is laying out the path provided by our salvation. It is the way that we, as followers of Jesus, can make our journey through this world. Our faith is in Christ crucified and raised from the dead, and therefore we, and all creation, are now reconciled with God. So as we are moving ever closer to our intended state of living in full communion with God, creation, and one another, we do so in the grace of God. It is in the knowledge of that grace and salvation that we can stand firm in the midst of every storm and crashing wave, enduring all kinds of hardship and suffering, because even then we know that "we have peace with God through our Lord Jesus Christ."

None of this removes the difficulty of the journey, but as discussed in previous chapters, this knowledge and confidence allow us to reframe, to reconsider what we have experienced and how we can move forward. Suffering can just as easily produce depression and defeat as it can endurance, perhaps even more easily. *How* is it that suffering can result in endurance and character and hope? When we enter into it with the prayer and the purpose of transformation. The mass shooting in the Tree of Life synagogue in Pittsburgh remains a tragedy. Yet the congregation also welcomed the grace and love of others into their lives. One year after the shooting, as they approached the High Holiday services, they were welcomed to worship in a local Episcopal church. As he seeks to lead his congregation and the larger Jewish community toward healing, Rabbi Myers says he begins each day with a question of God: "What do you want me to do?"[6]

Our own process of transformation began that night as Elizabeth and I drove back from the hospital and asked ourselves three questions: How will we love our daughter, remember our son, and continue to live? We had no idea. But we prayed and we asked of God, "What do you want us to do?" Moment by moment, we have been guided to opportunities and decisions that have enabled us to endure and to live. We have been blessed, even in the midst of our grief, but we are not unique or stronger or better than anyone else. Our loss remains, and so too does our suffering. But while it remains it becomes something more, something holy, something sacred, as we give it over to God.

Later in Romans, Paul further encourages us to make our way through this beautiful and terrible world by focusing on God's calling for us and committing to living for Christ: "To set the mind on the flesh is death, but to set the mind on the Spirit is life and peace" (Rom. 8:6). Paul is not advocating escapism, he is not saying to forget about the current struggles and trust that when you die you will be with Christ. While all of that is true, Paul is urging us to live fully in *this* life so that we might have the peace of Christ here and now, even as we continue to fight and struggle.

It was Jesus himself who promised us this means of overcoming the weight of the world: "Peace I leave with you; my peace I give to you. I do not give to you as the world gives. Do not let your hearts be troubled, and do not let them be afraid" (John 14:27). The peace of Christ is not the sort of peace politicians and diplomats rightly work for. It is not the cessation of violence or hardship, as much as those are the fruit of the Spirit at work in our lives. The peace of Christ is the knowledge that in spite of the violence and hardship, in spite of the suffering and grief, we are secure and safe in our Savior.

The peace of Christ means that although death remains a part of this life, it is no longer the final punishment of this world but simply the beginning of our full, complete, and eternal life. The peace of Christ is the knowledge and conviction, the sure hope, that "death has been swallowed up in victory" and that nothing can ever separate us from the love of God in Jesus Christ our Lord. And nothing will ever separate us again from those we love.

This book is *my* lament. It is my complaint to God that our son was taken from this life. It is not right, and it cannot be justified. This is also my declaration of thanksgiving as I remember God's presence throughout our lives, the grace and joy of Mack's birth, the mutual love of Mack and his sister, and the brilliant vibrancy of his life. It is a recounting of God's faithfulness to all creation and a confession of my faith in Christ. In lamenting the loss of Mack and affirming the grace of God present with us in the midst of our grief, I also call upon God to hear our prayers, the prayers of all who grieve and mourn, and to grant us the deep and abiding assurance of the hope of the resurrection: Be present and grant us your peace!

Amen. Come, Lord Jesus!
The grace of the Lord Jesus be with all the saints. Amen.
—Rev. 22:20–21

Reflection Questions

1. What does *hope* mean to you? What do you think of the idea that hope keeps people from facing struggles honestly, or as Nietzsche said, that it "prolongs [their] torment"?
2. Consider a commitment you entered into, perhaps a new job, a marriage, starting school, or having a child. What sustains you through the difficult times? What are the hopes and promises you felt as you began that journey?
3. Read Psalm 30. How does reflecting on your past experiences encourage you when looking to the future?

4. Revisit Romans 5:3–4 and the steps through which suffering transforms into hope. Have endurance and character been part of your grief journey? Consider your own grief, and reflect on how you would like to see it transformed.

5. What does *peace* mean to you? Consider a current moment of anxiety, strife, or conflict in your own life. Meditate on the fact that the peace of Christ is not the immediate end to conflict, but the assurance of Christ's presence and the *ultimate* resolution. How might you experience that peace in your life now?

PRAYERS OF COMFORT AND THANKSGIVING FROM *THE BOOK OF COMMON PRAYER*[1]

Merciful God, Father of our Lord Jesus Christ who is the Resurrection and the Life: Raise us, we humbly pray, from the death of sin to the life of righteousness; that when we depart this life we may rest in him, and at the resurrection receive that blessing which your well-beloved Son shall then pronounce: "Come, you blessed of my Father, receive the kingdom prepared for you from the beginning of the world." Grant this, O merciful Father, through Jesus Christ, our Mediator and Redeemer. *Amen.*

Grant, O Lord, to all who are bereaved the spirit of faith and courage, that we may have strength to meet the days to come with steadfastness and patience; not sorrowing as those without hope, but in thankful remembrance of your great goodness, and in the joyful expectation of eternal life with those we love. And this we ask in the Name of Jesus Christ our Savior. *Amen.*

NOTES

A word about endnotes, four words really: I don't like them. I find that endnotes interrupt the flow of reading, so while notes are useful for citing sources and sharing additional bits of information, they are not vital for the enjoyment and comprehension of the main text. Please feel free to wait until you have finished reading the chapter to check the notes. I promise you that they will still be there when you finish the chapter, and you will not miss anything!

Introduction

1. This book was given to me shortly after Mack died by my friend and scholar Gary Knoppers. Eric Wolterstorff had been Gary's roommate in college, and his death touched him deeply. Gary wanted to share with me the father's faithful reflections on death and grief. Shortly before Christmas 2018, Gary himself succumbed to cancer. He lived a full and wonderful life, leaving a tremendous legacy of family and scholarship, yet his days too were cut short.

Chapter 1: Letting It Out

1. Christian Brady, "The Will of God," *Targuman*, January 12, 2013, http://targuman.org/2013/01/12/the-will-of-god.

2. See Granger E. Westberg, *Good Grief* (Philadelphia: Fortress Press, 1962), 10–11.

3. Westberg, *Good Grief*, 16.

4. The Hebrew term *haśatan* means "the adversary." While we usually see it written as a name, "Satan," in this story we do not find the fallen angel of the Gospels but a divine being doing his appointed job: roaming the earth and bringing back to God a report about who deserves punishment. He is a sort of police officer and prosecuting attorney all rolled into one. God, knowing Job's great faithfulness, points him out to Satan who, quite reasonably, responds by pointing out that Job has been blessed with everything. Why would he not be faithful? If he had to suffer the normal hardships of life, he too would speak against God like other mortals. And so begins Job's woes.

5. The date of the book's composition has been placed anywhere from the tenth to the second century BCE; the linguistic evidence is inconclusive, and there is nothing internal to the text that would provide a firm historical setting. Most scholars argue that it is postexilic (sixth century), but it does have some similarities with much older Mesopotamian wisdom texts. There is a clear structural form, with the core poetic dialogues bracketed by a prose narrative (1:1–2:13; 42:7–17) that introduces and provides an explanation for Job's plight and then offers a dénouement. It is as likely that the prose was a shortened folk hero tale to which the poetry was added as an elaboration as it is that the narrative was added to an older poetic tradition; there is simply no sure way of knowing which was first. Regardless of the sources, it is this combined text that was preserved in the Jewish and Christian canons and comes down to us today.

6. See, for example, John Piper, "It Is Never Right to Be Angry with God," *Desiring God*, November 13, 2000, https://www.desiringgod.org/articles/it-is-never-right-to-be-angry-with-god.

7. Jerry A. Irish, *A Boy Thirteen: Reflections on Death* (Philadelphia: Westminster Press, 1975), 27.

8. Within ancient Judaism this was the common practice, to cite just a portion or even a few words of a passage in order to refer to the whole. It is found throughout texts from the Dead Sea Scrolls as well as the Mishnah and the Talmud.

9. Rather than having "anger toward God signif[ying] that [God] is bad or weak or cruel or foolish," as Piper suggests ("It Is Never Right"), our anger signifies that we have been hurt by our experience in this world. It is not a judgment about God but an expression of our feelings. Of course, Piper holds that all things in our lives have been

ordained by God; thus, we should never be upset about any calamity that befalls us, since God has designed it for our benefit and his glory. I do not believe that this is a biblical view.

10. "A Collect for Fridays," in *The Book Of Common Prayer and Administration of the Sacraments and Other Rites and Ceremonies of the Church: Together with the Psalter or Psalms of David According to the Use of the Episcopal Church* (New York: Seabury Press, 1979), 99. (Hereafter, this work will be abbreviated *BCP*.) A "collect" (pronounced *kah-leckt*) is a short prayer often said at the beginning and end of services. Each chapter will end with such a short prayer as a reflection and benediction. If there is no citation, the collect is original to this work.

Chapter 2: Here Is the World

1. Max Roser, Hannah Ritchie, and Bernadeta Dadonaite, "Child and Infant Mortality," Our World in Data, https://ourworldindata.org/child-mortality.

2. These examples are Rachel in Gen. 35:16–20, and the wife of Phinehas and mother of Ichabod (sadly, we do not know her name) in 1 Sam. 4:20.

3. Robert Alter, *The Hebrew Bible: A Translation with Commentary*, vol. 3, *The Writings* (New York: W. W. Norton & Co., 2019), 675.

4. This is Alter's rendering of the Hebrew *hevel hevelim*.

5. Bart D. Ehrman, *God's Problem: How the Bible Fails to Answer Our Most Important Question — Why We Suffer* (San Francisco: HarperOne, 2008), 192.

6. Ehrman, *God's Problem*, 189.

7. C. S. Lewis, *The Problem of Pain* (New York: Macmillan, 1947), 21–22.

8. This is precisely the position of John Piper. See Piper, "The Suffering of Christ and the Sovereignty of God," in *Suffering and the Sovereignty of God*, ed. John Piper and Justin Taylor (Wheaton, IL: Crossway Books, 2006), 81–89. "According to this divine plan, God permits sin to enter the world. God ordains that what he hates will come to pass. It is not sin in God to will that there be sin" (85). The logic of that last sentence escapes me.

9. D. A. Carson, *How Long, O Lord? Reflections on Suffering and Evil* (Grand Rapids, MI: Baker Academic, 2006), 179.

Chapter 3: The Why of Suffering

1. Michele Norris, "Father Recalls Deadly Blast At Ala. Baptist Church," NPR, September 15, 2008, https://www.npr.org/templates /story/story.php?storyId=94640715.

2. Ken Williams, "Toward a Biblical Theology of Suffering," *International Training Partners*, http://www.relationshipskills.com/resources /Toward-a-Theology-of-Suffering.pdf.

3. Nicholas Wolterstorff, *Lament for a Son* (Grand Rapids: Eerdmans, 2009), 74.

4. G. K. Chesterton, *Heretics* (London, New York: John Lane, 1905), 79.

5. See Genesis 4. In chapter 5 we learn that Cain found a woman, married, and had children. A reasonable question is, Whom did Cain marry? Yet it is not a question that the Bible is concerned with and so does not provide an answer. It is a good reminder that we should not ask of the text questions for which it cannot provide answers.

6. Nick Corasaniti, Richard Pérez-Peña, and Lizette Alvarez, "Church Massacre Suspect Held as Charleston Grieves," *New York Times*, June 19, 2015, https://www.nytimes.com/2015/06/19/us/charleston -church-shooting.html.

7. Jaweed Kaleem, "South Carolina Lutheran Pastor: Dylann Roof Was Church Member, His Family Prays for Victims," *Huffington Post*, June 19, 2015, https://www.huffingtonpost.com/2015/06/19/dylann -roof-religion-church-lutheran_n_7623990.html.

8. Polly Mosendz, "Dylann Roof Confesses: Says He Wanted to Start 'Race War,'" *Newsweek*, June 19, 2015, https://www.newsweek .com/dylann-roof-confesses-church-shooting-says-he-wanted-start-race -war-344797.

9. According to Gun Violence Archive (https://www.gun violencearchive.org), a "mass shooting" is defined as a shooting in which four or more people are shot, not including the gunman. Since 2013, there have been more than 2,000 mass shootings in the United States.

10. "Bishop of Truro's Independent Review for the Foreign Secretary of FCO Support for Persecuted Christians," https://christian persecutionreview.org.uk/interim-report/.

11. "Genocide," United Nations Office on Genocide Prevention and the Responsibility to Protect, https://www.un.org/en/genocide prevention/genocide.shtml.

Chapter 4: "The Remainder"

1. Wolterstorff, *Lament for a Son*, 74.

2. James L. Crenshaw, "Book of Job," in *The Anchor Bible Dictionary*, vol. 3, ed. David Noel Freedman (New York: Doubleday, 1992), 862. This article is an excellent introduction to the critical and interpretive issues of the book of Job.

3. Alter has essentially the same rendering as the Jewish Publication Society's *Tanakh: The Holy Scriptures: The New JPS Translation according to the Traditional Hebrew Text* (Philadelphia: Jewish Publication Society, 1985). Alter's translation is, "Therefore do I recant, and I repent in dust and ashes" (Alter, *The Hebrew Bible*, 577).

4. "Prayer for Guidance," *BCP*, 832.

Chapter 5: One Step

1. C. S. Lewis, *A Grief Observed* (New York: Seabury Press, 1961), 43.

2. "Catechism," *BCP*, 857.

3. There are variations of the poem circulating, and authorship is disputed, with at least four people claiming to be the author: Burrell Webb, Mary Stevenson, Margaret Fishback Powers, and Carolyn Joyce Carty.

4. "Holy Eucharist, Rite II, Prayer A," *BCP*, 362.

5. "A Collect for Fridays," *BCP*, 99.

Chapter 6: Walking in Grace

1. For example: "God does not merely passively permit such things [as the Holocaust or cancer or any kind of suffering] by standing by and not stopping them. Rather, he actively wills them by ordaining them and then bringing them about, yet without himself thereby becoming the author of sin." Mark Talbot, "'All the Good That Is Ours in Christ': Seeing God's Gracious Hand in the Hurts Others Do to Us,"

in *Suffering and the Sovereignty of God*, ed. John Piper and Justin Taylor (Wheaton, IL: Crossway Books, 2006), 35.

2. John Piper and David Powlison, "Don't Waste Your Cancer," in Piper and Taylor, *Suffering and the Sovereignty of God*, 207.

3. Bart Ehrman, *God's Problem: How the Bible Fails to Answer Our Most Important Question—Why We Suffer* (San Francisco: HarperOne, 2008), 3.

4. Carson, *How Long, O Lord?*, 65–66.

5. I was "locally formed," which means that I did not go off to seminary. My theological background and degrees were deemed significant enough that local, practical experience in addition to examinations was deemed sufficient.

6. "[If] we see such suffering as, in the first place, the effluent of the fall, the result of a fallen world, the consequence of evil that is really evil and in which we ourselves all too frequently indulge, then however much we may grieve when we suffer, we will not be taken by surprise." Carson, *How Long, O Lord?*, 45.

7. Viktor E. Frankl, *Man's Search for Meaning* (Pocket Books, 1985), 99.

8. Kelly M. Kapic, *Embodied Hope: A Theological Meditation on Pain and Suffering* (Downers Grove, IL: IVP Academic, 2017).

9. "Exercise Is an All-Natural Treatment to Fight Depression," *Harvard Health Letter*, updated April 30, 2018, https://www.health.harvard.edu/mind-and-mood/exercise-is-an-all-natural-treatment-to-fight-depression.

10. "A Collect for Guidance," *BCP*, 100.

Chapter 7: Living in the Moment

1. The "Mourners Kaddish" is recited by the congregation in the synagogue, with a *minyan* (a quorum of ten men, or in some cases men and women, over the age of thirteen needed for worship and prayer):

Glorified and sanctified be God's great name throughout the world
which He has created according to His will.
May He establish His kingdom in your lifetime and during your days,

and within the life of the entire House of Israel, speedily
and soon;
and say, *Amen.*
May His great name be blessed forever and to all eternity.
Blessed and praised, glorified and exalted, extolled and
honored,
adored and lauded be the name of the Holy One, blessed
be He,
beyond all the blessings and hymns, praises and consolations
that
are ever spoken in the world; and say, *Amen.*
May there be abundant peace from heaven, and life, for us
and for all Israel; and say, *Amen.*
He who creates peace in His celestial heights,
may He create peace for us and for all Israel;
and say, *Amen.*

2. "A Collect for the Renewal of Life, *BCP*, 99.

3. "A Collect for Proper 12, the Sunday closest to July 27," *BCP*, 231.

Chapter 8: Raised Imperishable

1. It is also the root of much of rabbinic commentary called *midrash*. The rabbis looked for these gaps and sought to fill them in based upon speculation and various other exegetical tools.

2. *Seeking God Winks* (blog), July 30, 2019, http://seekinggodwinks .blogspot.com/2019/07/july-30.html.

3. N. T. Wright, *The Resurrection of the Son of God* (Minneapolis: Fortress Press, 2003). The greatest strength of this excellent work is Wright's proper rooting of the understanding of the resurrection in the Jewish context. See also the engaging interview with Wright by David Van Biema, "Christians Wrong about Heaven, Says Bishop," *Time*, February 7, 2008, http://content.time.com/time/world/article /0,8599,1710844,00.html.

4. Van Biema, "Christians Wrong about Heaven, Says Bishop."

5. Wright, *Resurrection of the Son of God*, 216. See also N. T. Wright, *Surprised by Hope: Rethinking Heaven, the Resurrection, and the Mission of the Church* (Grand Rapids, MI: Zondervan, 2010).

6. Wright makes a distinction between this "restful happiness" and "soul sleep," but his argument seems to me largely a distinction without a difference: "Though this is sometimes described as 'sleep,' we shouldn't take this to mean that it is a state of unconsciousness. Had Paul thought that, I very much doubt that he would have described life immediately after death as 'being with Christ, which is far better.' Rather, 'sleep' here means that the body is 'asleep' in the sense of 'dead,' while the real person—however we want to describe him or her—continues." Wright, *Surprised by Hope*, 183. I would not say that I think Wright is wrong, but that there is room for other interpretations of Scripture.

7. That is assuming you take the most conservative view of his likely time frame, c. 1800 BCE.

8. An excellent place to begin learning about Brunner is Alister E. McGrath, *Emil Brunner: A Reappraisal* (Oxford: Wiley-Blackwell, 2016).

9. Brunner, *Eternal Hope*, 153.

10. Brunner, *Eternal Hope*, 151.

11. Brunner, *Eternal Hope*, 154.

12. This is the *Pascha Nostrum*, an ancient Christian hymn sung at Easter that is comprised of 1 Cor. 5:7–8, Rom. 6:9–11, and 1 Cor. 15:20–22.

Chapter 9: The Already and the Not Yet

1. J. R. R. Tolkien, *The Fellowship of the Ring: Being the First Part of the Lord of the Rings* (London: Unwin Paperbacks, 1979), 78.

2. The more painful question was whether or not we should have an open casket. I was against it, but Glen, the funeral home director, advised it, saying that it has been shown to help children fully come to terms with the fact that their friend has really died and has not just "gone away." He was right.

3. This entire vision is full of the Hebrew particle for "like" or "as," since the author doesn't want his audience to be confused and think that God is actually any of these things. It is all simile, and that point is driven home through the sheer weight of repetition.

4. "U2 October Interview 1982," YouTube, https://www.youtube.com/watch?v=4oCslM0tXKI.

5. "Collect of the Day" for Holy Saturday (adapted), *BCP*, 221.

Chapter 10: Hope

1. Barry P. Powell, *The Poems of Hesiod: Theogony, Works and Days, and the Shield of Herakles* (Oakland: University Press of California, 2017), 112.

2. Friedrich Nietzsche, *Human, All-Too-Human: Parts One and Two*, trans. Helen Zimmern and Paul V. Cohn (Mineola, NY: Dover Publications, 2006), 53. By enabling Pandora to close the jar with hope remaining within, Nietzsche argues, Zeus kept hope ever tantalizingly close to humanity: "Now for ever man has the casket of happiness in his house and thinks he holds a great treasure; it is at his disposal, he stretches out his hand for it whenever he desires; for he does not know the box which Pandora brought was the casket of evil, and he believes the ill which remains within to be the greatest blessing, it is hope" (53).

3. Emil Brunner, *Eternal Hope* (Philadelphia: Westminster Press, 1954), 7.

4. "The Celebration and Blessing of Marriage," *BCP*, 423.

5. Frederick Buechner, "Grace," in *Beyond Words: Daily Reading in the ABCs of Faith* (San Francisco: HarperOne, 2004), 139.

6. Mike Kelly, "Tree of Life: How Can a Community Heal after a Mass Shooting? A Rabbi Searches for Answers," *USA Today*, October 27, 2019, https://news.yahoo.com/tree-life-community-heal-mass-090008 566.html.

Prayers of Comfort and Thanksgiving from *The Book of Common Prayer*

1. "The Burial of the Dead: Rite Two," *BCP*, 505.